THE
CHURCH
CONFRONTS
THE NAZIS

THE CHURCH CONFRONTS THE NAZIS:

BARMEN

THEN AND NOW

Edited by
HUBERT G. LOCKE

Toronto Studies in Theology
Volume 16

The Edwin Mellen Press
New York and Toronto

THE CHURCH CONFRONTS THE NAZIS:
BARMEN THEN AND NOW
Edited by Hubert G. Locke

ISBN 0-88946-762-5

Toronto Studies in Theology
Series ISBN 0-88946-975-X

dedicated to the memory of

WILHELM NIEMÖLLER

historian of the German church struggle

ACKNOWLEDGEMENTS

In addition to the efforts of those who prepared the major essays for this volume, the work of Thelma Brown, Linda Christian, Lucia Enriquez and Andrea Menin who diligently typed the manuscripts and Dr. Warren Lewis who provided exceptionally skilled editorial and counsel is gratefully acknowledged.

CONTENTS

INTRODUCTION

The essays in this volume were prepared as working papers for the International Symposium of Scholars and Church Leaders in Seattle, April 24-29, 1984. The theme of the Symposium--<u>A Half-Century After Barmen: Religion, Totalitarianism, and Human Freedom in the Modern World</u>--reflects the occasion for the convening of the week-long series of addresses and discussions. It marks the fiftieth anniversary of a little-known but momentous event in the life of the German churches during the fateful, twelve-year period of the German Third Reich.

When Adolf Hitler and the National Socialist German Workers (Nazi) Party came to power on January 30, 1933, Hitler set out to align every single facet of German society with the principles and programs of Nazism. Among those principles were a fanatical loyalty to the personal, absolute authority of Hitler himself; a fierce hatred of communism and the Jewish populace; and blind belief in the notion that the German people constituted a superior or "master" race of human beings. Almost immediately, Hitler ran into pockets of opposition from the German churches, both Catholic and Protestant. The opposition was not always for the noblest of reasons and, in the case of German Catholicism, was officially cut short barely five months after Hitler came to power when the Vatican signed a Concordat--or treaty--with the Nazi government. Resistance continued, however, among individual Catholics and by an organized segment of the Protestant churches. That resistance constitutes the remarkable story of the Church Struggle in Nazi Germany. In those moments when the German churches and their leaders spoke out with force and clarity--as they did at Barmen on May 29-31, 1934--their judgments stand as one of the few, public denunciations of Hitler and Nazism to be heard from within Germany during the awful years, 1933-1945.

I

On May 24-31, 1934, one hundred thirty-nine delegates of the German Evangelical Church, representing the Lutheran, Reformed, and United church confessions, met in the town of Barmen--now a suburb of the industrial city of Wuppertal in the Ruhr Valley. There they unanimously approved a six-point Declaration, drafted by the famed theologian, Karl Barth, in which they took pointed issue with some of the fundamental tenets of Nazi philosophy. The Barmen Declaration--as it has come to be called--was primarily directed to those German church leaders who were passionate supporters of Hitler and Nazism. Its language is theological, its format a set of brief commentaries on six biblical passages, and its tone strident in its rejection of what was perceived to be the "false doctrine"¯ promulgated by the church devotees of Hitler. But in the context of the times, it was also a ringing political statement, in spite of the efforts of those responsible for it to deny this fact. The subsequent events in the history of the Church Struggle proved as much.

Article One of the Declaration is a direct assault on the Nazi "Führerprinzip"--the idea as expressed by Hitler himself, that decisions in the Nazi State would be "made by one man....only he alone may possess the authority and the right to command."[1] In response, the Barmen Declaration quoted the Gospel of St. John (14:1), "I am the way, the truth, and the life," and then stated its rejection of the idea that the Church could acknowledge any other "events, powers, figures, and truths as God's revelation." This first article took on added significance, eleven days after the session at Barmen ended, when a group of professors and clergy issued a counterstatement which declared "...the unchangeable will of God...binds everyone...to the natural orders to which we are subject, such as family, nation, race....In this knowledge we thank God the Lord that he has given to our people in its need a Leader [i.e. Hitler] as a 'pious and faithful sovereign.'"

Such was the character of the Barmen Declaration and the controversy it stirred,

both within the churches and the Nazi State.
Its five other Articles were equally
provocative, challenging the notions that
Christians could be loyal to anyone other
than Christ, that the Church could recast its
teachings to fit "prevailing ideological and
political convictions," that the State could
become "the single and totalitarian order of
human life," and that the Church could place
itself in the service of any human "desires,
purposes, and plans." No one, reading the
Declaration in 1934, could fail to see that
it spoke as forcefully against the principles
underlying Nazism and the government of
Adolph Hitler as it did to those in churches
who gave their enthusiastic endorsement to
those principles and to the government.

The subsequent course of events in the
Church Struggle are the subject of two of the
essays in this volume. They describe the
formal rift within the German Evangelical
Church which occurred after the Barmen
Declaration was published, the escalation of
violence by the state against the church
leaders who espoused the Barmen principles,
the gradual weakening of resistance from
within the churches under the impact of state

pressures, and the ultimate failure of the
Nazi State to crush completely this organized
center of opposition to its aims.

As for the Barmen Declaration itself, it
is now considered--a half-century later-- to
rank "among the great Creeds and Confessions
of the Christian Church." Adopted in various
forms in the constitutions of several
Lutheran and Reformed churches in Germany
after the war and by the United Presbyterian
Church (USA) in 1967, the Declaration, as its
foremost American interpreter, Arthur
Cochrane, has noted, "...has exerted an
influence beyond the role it played in the
Church struggle in Germany, 1934-1935."

II

Two important caveats are to be kept in
mind when dealing with historical events from
the past. The first warns us against the
peril of making historical comparisons, which
often are awkward at best, or, at worst, may
lead to distortion of the uniqueness which
resides in every historical situation. The
second reminds us, as the philosopher

Santayana once stated, that those who do not
learn from history are condemned to repeat
it.

   Somewhere between these two cautions, we
are obliged to sift the record of the German
Church Struggle and to search out whatever
lessons it may hold for our era. This is
essentially the purpose of the International
Symposium. Its title was deliberately chosen
to suggest that we engage not only in a
searching analysis of the events in the life
of the German churches from 1933 to 1945, but
also that we ask what insights, challenges,
and warnings they may contain for the life of
the Church today, as it confronts the problem
of totalitarianism and the concern for human
liberty in the modern world.

   There are, to be sure, enormous
differences between Germany during the period
of the Third Reich and modern nation-states
today. Germany, like all societies, has its
own unique history, traditions, customs, and
culture; to ignore those unique features of
German life is to misread the German
historical record badly. Likewise, the
German Protestant churches--both in the

period 1933-1934 and today--are remarkably unlike the history, traditions, and structural forms of Protestantism in most other Western nations. The reflection of German feudalism, the impact of the Reformation, the peculiarities of a state-supported religion, and other significant factors in the history of the German church are particularities of Germany's religious life oft-times difficult for non-Germans to understand.

Vast differences notwithstanding, it is equally perilous to ignore certain similarities between circumstances and events in the Germany of fifty years ago and our own era. Germany was a nation beset by the economic depression that gripped most of the Western world in the 1930's. It was a country desperate to reclaim the military prowess it had lost in World War I and with it a deceptive loss of national pride and honor. It was a society pervaded by an inchoate paranoia about communism and with a long-standing, deeply-rooted prejudice against its Jewish minority. Many of its church leaders bemoaned the loss of family virtues and the old morality that ostensibly had characterized German life in days past.

Into such a social and economic climate came Hitler and the Nazis--first as a radical, vociferous minority, but increasingly as a voice of power in German politics. Hitler and the Nazi Party played on every fear and appealed to every misguided instinct in the German populace. Thoughtful Germans refused to take Hitler and his party seriously: business leaders thought Hitler could be manipulated to their own advantage and the military maintained a deep-seated suspicion until they saw that support for the new regime meant an aggressive build-up of arms and military preparedness. But millions of Germans fervently believed that both Hitler and the Nazi Party were the answer to Germany's woes as well as their salvation for the future. Twelve years later, the entire world had experienced the most destructive military conflict in the history of warfare, Germany lay in rubble, six million European Jews had been systematically put to death, and five million other European civilians ruthlessly exterminated.

III

Arthur Cochrane wrote <u>The Church's</u> <u>Confession Under Hitler</u>, which still ranks as the major work in English dealing with the history of the Synod of Barmen and its Declaration. On October 31, 1974 Cochrane gave an address at Princeton University to mark the fortieth anniversary of Barmen and the four hundred fifty-seventh anniversary of the Reformation. In that address, he quoted Karl Barth who, after the war, acknowledged that while both the Barmen Synod and the Confessing Church to which it gave rise could be reproached for having fought against National Socialism on too narrow a front, they nevertheless managed to accomplish far more in their opposition to the Nazis than did all the other groups and institutions in German society--the universities, the legal profession, business, theatre and art, the army and the trade unions. Cochrane himself suggested that

Barmen has provided a correct and exemplary starting-point for the Church's witness in regard to racial,

social, political and economic
questions....In the face of the war in
Vietnam, of racial, social, and economic
injustice, of corruption in the
government and the judicial system, not
to speak of a pseudo-Christian White
House religion, has not the weakness of
the Church in America taken its mobility
to speak as a <u>Church</u>--as a Church sure
of its authority and freedom, its own
nature and task?[2]

Cochrane wrote in 1974. Now, a decade later,
with the Barmen Declaration and the
experience of the German Church Struggle as
the most powerfully compelling guideposts in
recent times, we still search in America for
answers to this relentless question. The
search goes on elsewhere as well--in Poland
and South Africa, for example--but in the
United States today, this quest has several
dimensions.

In spite of the conventional wisdom that
religion and politics do not mix well, or the
frequently-heard assertion that "politics
should be kept out of the pulpit," American

society has a long and time-honored tradition of its religious leaders engaging in the political life and issues of the nation. Puritan preachers in the 18th century provided fervent spiritual support to the ideas of freedom and liberty that helped to inspire the War of Independence. Both conservative and liberal clergy in the 19th century brought the weight of their moral indignation to bear in the anti-slavery movement. In our own era we need only recall the passionate speeches and sermons of Martin Luther King, Jr. in the civil rights movement of the 1960's, or the relentless efforts of the two brothers-priests, Daniel and Phillip Berrigan, in the Vietnam War era. These three stand for a legion of American pastors and priests and laypersons for whom religion and its implications for the social, economic, and political issues of their time are inseparable.

But if this is part of the legacy of American religion, it is also part of the problem! For every Puritan preacher who supported the colonial struggle for independence, there was at least one who supported the British side of the issue. For every Charles Finney and Phillips Brooks who championed the emancipation of slaves, an equal--if not greater--number proclaimed from the pulpit that slavery was the will of God. And in our own era, for every cleric who supports equal rights for women or nuclear disarmament, other clerics will be found who denounce the Equal Rights Amendment as a sign of moral rot in the nation and who proclaim that the nuclear disarmament movement is a communist conspiracy.

How do we weigh these competing and conflicting messages--all of which purport to speak with divine authority? Which message and messenger is authentic? How are we to determine which, within the babble of religious voices we hear, is genuinely the voice of God, rather than a composite of attitudes, opinions, or biases of individuals or groups, speaking under the cloak of religion--whether liberal or conservative?

The one hundred thirty-nine delegates at the Barmen Synod wrestled, albeit in a different context, with essentially the same set of questions. Both supporters of Hitler and Nazi ideology and those who denounced the regime and its leader claimed to be faithful to the will of God. Both sides claimed the testimony of scripture and creeds in support of their positions. But one of the uniquenesses of Barmen was its unrelenting commitment to speak as a church--as the earnest, thoughtful, prayerfully considered convictions of chosen leaders of the Christian community, acting out of the deepest concern for the integrity and authenticity of the Church's witness and message.

To place the problem in its modern context, the Barmen Declaration was not the message of either an ecumenical commission or a TV evangelist. It was neither editorial opinion nor a self-inspired denominational position paper. It was the outcome of three full days of prayer, worship, and discussion among one hundred thirty-nine carefully chosen representatives of eighteen of the twenty-seven provincial Churches of Germany, who reflected the widest possible geographical, theological, and professional backgrounds. Fifty-three of the one hundred thirty-nine delegates were laypersons--engineers, publishers,

physicists, businessmen, lawyers, physicians,
book dealers, architects, social
workers....even a tax collector! Together
with bishops, pastors, and theological
professors, they constituted a core of the
Church's (and Germany's) best leadership.
But it was not their intellectual acumen or
professorial stature that produced the Barmen
Declaration. It was--as stated in the
opening lines of the Declaration itself and
addressed as "an appeal to the Evangelical
Congregations and Christians in
Germany"--their search, for "a common message
for the need and temptation of the Church in
our day" and their conviction that they had
been given "a common word to utter" that has
given our century one of the most powerful
statements of Christian faith in its
relationship to the issues of its day.

IV

The two final essays in this volume seek
to address those issues of our time which the
Church presently confronts and on which
voices within the Church are seriously
divided. One is authored by a church-man;

the other, by a scholar without church affiliation but with a careful respect for the role of religion in the modern world. Neither seeks to offer answers or alternatives, but only to raise questions that ought to be at the forefront of the Church's faith in its struggle with contemporary circumstances.

A companion volume, consisting of the major addresses given at the 1984 International Symposium, will be published subsequently. This volume serves as a brief introduction to the history of the Barmen Synod, its Declaration, and the struggle of the German churches which was one of its outcomes. As Professor Cochrane wrote in the first edition of his work:

> A study of the nature and history of the Barmen Theological Declaration naturally prompts questions in the minds of the student. What is the likelihood of something like Barmen happening in other countries... Are we living "between the times?" Were those twelve terrible yet blessed years of the Church under Hitler a foreshadowing of the destiny of the

Church in other lands in this atomic age? ...Are we on the threshold of a day when the Church knows that its only weapons and defenses will be its Confession of Faith? Are we conscious of some great heresy by which our Churches are "grievously imperiled" and of some great truth by which we are possessed? Are we prepared to make dogmatic and, much more important, ethical decisions as a Church, and for the sake of them to lose our life in order to find it?

These remain, for serious Christian adherents, the compelling questions of our age and every age.

Hubert G. Locke

Footnotes

[1] From <u>Mein Kampf</u>, 1943 English translation, pp. 449-50.

[2] "The Theology of Barmen," Appendix XI in the 2nd Edition of <u>The Church's Confession Under Hitler</u> (1976), pp. 280-281.

TEXT OF THE BARMEN DECLARATION

I. An Appeal to the Evangelical Congregations and Christians in Germany

The Confessional Synod of the German Evangelical Church met in Barmen, May 29-31, 1934. Here representatives from all the German Confessional Churches met with one accord in a confession of the one Lord of the one, holy, apostolic Church. In fidelity to their Confession of Faith, members of Lutheran, Reformed, and United Churches sought a common message for the need and temptation of the Church in our day. With gratitude to God they are convinced that they have been given a common word to utter. It was not their intention to found a new Church or to form a union. For nothing was farther from their minds than the abolition of the confessional status of our Churches. Their intention was, rather, to withstand in faith and unanimity the destruction of the Confession of Faith, and thus of the Evangelical Church in Germany. In opposition to attempts to establish the unity of the German Evangelical Church by means of false doctrine, by the use of force and insincere practices, the Confessional Synod insists that the unity of the Evangelical Churches in Germany can come only from the Word of God in faith through the Holy Spirit. Thus alone is the Church renewed.

Therefore the Confessional Synod calls upon the congregations to range themselves behind it in prayer, and steadfastly to gather around those pastors and teachers who are loyal to the Confessions.

Be not deceived by loose talk, as if we meant to oppose the unity of the German nation! Do not listen to the seducers who

pervert our intentions, as if we wanted to
break up the unity of the German Evangelical
Church or to forsake the Confessions of the
Fathers!

Try the spirits whether they are of God!
Prove also the words of the Confessional
Synod of the German Evangelical Church to see
whether they agree with Holy Scripture and
with the Confessions of the Fathers. If you
find that we are speaking contrary to
Scripture, then do not listen to us! But if
you find that we are taking our stand upon
Scripture, then let no fear or temptation
keep you from treading with us the path of
faith and obedience to the Word of God, in
order that God's people be of one mind upon
earth and that we in faith experience what he
himself has said: "I will never leave, nor
forsake you." Therefore, "Fear not, little
flock, for it is your Father's good pleasure
to give you the kingdom."

II.   Theological Declaration Concerning the
Present Situation of the German
Evangelical Church

According to the opening words of its
constitution of July 11, 1933, the German
Evangelical Church is a federation of
Confessional Churches that grew out of the
Reformation and that enjoy equal rights. The
theological basis for the unification of
these Churches is laid down in Article 1 and
Article 2(1) of the constitution of the
German Evangelical Church that was recognized
by the Reich Government on July 14, 1933:

Article 1. The inviolable founda-
tion of the German Evangelical
Church is the gospel of Jesus
Christ as it is attested for us in
Holy Scripture and brought to light

again in the Confessions of the
Reformation. The full powers that
the Church needs for its missions
are hereby determined and limited.
Article 2(1). The German Evangelical Church is divided into member
Churches (Landeskirchen).

We, the representatives of Lutheran,
Reformed, and United Churches, of free
synods, Church assemblies, and parish
organizations united in the Confessional
Synod of the German Evangelical Church,
declare that we stand together on the ground
of the German Evangelical Church as a
federation of German Confessional Churches.
We are bound together by the confession of
the one Lord of the one, holy, catholic, and
apostolic Church.

We publicly declare before all
evangelical Churches in German that what they
hold in common in this Confession is
grievously imperiled, and with it the unity
of the German Evangelical Church. It is
threatened by the teaching methods and
actions of the ruling Church party of the
"German Christians" and of the Church
administration carried on by them. These
have become more and more apparent during the
first year of the existence of the German
Evangelical Church. This threat consists in
the fact that the theological basis, in which
the German Evangelical Church is united, has
been continually and systematically thwarted
and rendered ineffective by alien principles,
on the part of the leaders and spokesmen of
the "German Christians" as well as on the
part of the Church administration. When
these principles are held to be valid, then,
according to all the Confessions in force
among us, the Church ceases to be the Church,
and the German Evangelical Church, as a

federation of the Confessional Churches, becomes intrinsically impossible.

As members of Lutheran, Reformed, and United Churches we may and must speak with one voice in this matter today. Precisely because we want to be and to remain faithful to our various Confessions, we may not keep silent, since we believe that we have been given a common message to utter in a time of common need and temptation. We commend to God what this may mean for the interrelations of the Confessional Churches.

In view of the errors of the "German Christians" of the present Reich Church government which are devastating the Church and are also thereby breaking up the unity of the German Evangelical Church, we confess the following evangelical truths:

1. "I am the way, and the truth, and the life; no one comes to the Father, but by me." (John 14:6) "Truly, truly, I say to you, he who does not enter the sheepfold by the door but climbs in by another way, that man is a thief and a robber...I am the door; if anyone enters by me, he will be saved." (John 10:1,9.)

Jesus Christ, as he is attested for us in Holy Scripture, is the one Word of God which we have to hear and which we have to trust and obey in life and in death.

We reject the false doctrine, as though the Church could and would have to acknowledge as a source of its proclamation, apart from and besides this one Work of God, still other events and powers, figures and truths, as God's revelation.

2. "Christ Jesus, whom God made our wisdom, our righteousness and sanctification and redemption." (I Cor. 1:30.)

As Jesus Christ is God's assurance of the forgiveness of all our sins, so in the same way and with the same seriousness he is also God's mighty claim upon our whole life. Through him befalls us a joyful deliverance from the godless fetters of this world for a free, grateful service to his creatures.

We reject the false doctrine, as though there were areas of our life in which we would not belong to Jesus Christ, but to other lords -- areas in which we would not need justification and sanctification through him.

3. "Rather, speaking the truth in love, we are to grow up in every way into him who is the head, into Christ, from whom the whole body [is] joined and knit together." (Eph. 4:15-16.)

The Christian Church is the congregation of the brethren in which Jesus Christ acts presently as the Lord in Word and sacrament through the Holy Spirit. As the Church of pardoned sinners, it has to testify in the midst of a sinful world, with its faith as with its obedience, with its message as with its order, that it is solely his property, and that it lives and wants to live solely from his comfort and from his direction in the expectation of his appearance.

We reject the false doctrine, as though the Church were permitted to abandon the form of its message and order to its own pleasure or to changes in prevailing ideological and political convictions.

4. "You know that the rulers of the Gentiles lord it over them, and their great men exercise authority over them. It shall not be so among you; but whoever would be great among you must be your servant." (Matt. 20:25-26.)

The various offices in the Church do not establish a dominion of some over others; on the contrary, they are for the exercise of the ministry entrusted to and enjoined upon the whole congregation.

We reject the false doctrine, as though the Church, apart from this ministry, could and were permitted to give to itself, or allow to be given to it, special leaders vested with ruling powers.

5. "Fear God. Honor the emperor." (I Peter 2:17.)

Scripture tells us that, in the as yet unredeemed world in which the Church also exists, the State has by divine appointment, the task of providing for justice and peace. [It fulfills this task] by means of the threat and exercise of force, according to the measure of human judgment and human ability. The Church acknowledges the benefit of this divine appointment in gratitude and reverence before him. It calls to mind the Kingdom of God, God's commandment and righteousness, and thereby the responsibility both of rulers and of the ruled. It trusts and obeys the power of the Word by which God upholds all things.

We reject the false doctrine, as though the State, over and beyond its special commission, should and could become the single and totalitarian order of human life, thus fulfilling the Church's vocation as well.

We reject the false doctrine, as though
the Church, over and beyond its special
commission, should and could appropriate the
characteristics, the tasks, and the dignity
of the State, thus itself becoming an organ
of the State.

6. "Lo, I am with you always, to the
close of the age." (Matt. 28:20.) "The word
of God is not fettered." (II Tim. 2:9)

The Church's commission, upon which its
freedom is founded, consists in delivering
the message of the free grace of God to all
people in Christ's stead, and therefore in
the ministry of his own Word and work through
sermon and sacrament.

We reject the false doctrine, as though
the Church in human arrogance could place the
Word and work of the Lord in the service of
any arbitrarily chosen desires, purposes, and
plans.

The Confessional Synod of the German
Evangelical Church declares that it sees in
the acknowledgement of these truths and in
the rejection of these errors the
indispensable theological basis of the German
Evangelical Church as a federation of the
Confessional Churches. It invites all who
are able to accept its declaration to be
mindful of these theological principles in
their decisions in Church politics. It
entreats all whom it concerns to return to
the unity of faith, love, and hope.

THE BARMEN SYNOD AND ITS DECLARATION: A HISTORICAL SYNOPSIS

- Robert P. Ericksen

"Our Protestant churches have greeted the German turning point of 1933 as a gift and miracle of God."[1] With these words Paul Althaus, highly respected professor of theology at Erlangen University and president of the Luther Society for thirty years, welcomed the rise of Adolf Hitler and the Nazi Party. His works confront us with the unplesant and perhaps unexpected fact that most church leaders and church members in Germany welcomed Hitler. Althaus went on to say, "We accept the turning point of this year as mercy from God's hand."[2] A proclamation from the Bavarian church synod echoed Althaus:

> A state which begins again to rule according to God's law deserves not only the applause but also the joyous and active collaboration of the church.[3]

In retrospect this latter sentiment seems based on a huge misunderstanding. Did Hitler rule according to God's law? Since 1945 we have learned to recognize Hitler as one of the most powerful symbols of evil in modern times. We might like to assume this would have been apparent to Christians in Germany, and that they would have resisted his rule. Indeed, a few examples of resistance can be cited. Martin Niemöller, a Lutheran pastor, was arrested by the Gestapo in 1937 and spent the next eight years in a concentration camp. Another Lutheran pastor, Dietrich Bonhöffer, was executed for his participation in a plot against Hitler's life. We also recognize the Barmen Declaration, supported by both Niemöller and Bonhöffer, as a statement of church opposition to the Nazi regime; and there developed in Germany a "Confessing Church," based upon the Barmen Declaration. Does this evidence show that Christians in Germany opposed Hitler? The simple answer is no. The best answer to this question, however, is more complicated.

A close look at church leaders and theologians in Germany reveals a very broad range of responses to the Nazi era. A few opposed Hitler's politics. A large number supported Hitler's politics but opposed his church politics. For example, some Confessing Church members religiously faithful to the Barmen Declaration were also active Stormtroopers. And some Christians in Germany believed that the Protestant church and Nazi Party should march hand in hand. This latter group, the "German Christians," attempted to take over the Protestant church in 1933. Their extremism in both theology and tactics prompted the Barmen Declaration and the "Church Struggle."

We appropriately celebrate the fiftieth anniversary of the Barmen Declaration and rightly admire the courageous supporters of

Barmen in 1934. Nevertheless, we must look carefully at the Barmen Synod and Declaration in order to see more than a simple picture of good guys versus bad guys. This effort leads us into an intricate web of national politics, church politics and theology, and it confronts us with the realization that the church simply did not effectively meet the challenge of the Nazi era.

THE CRISIS OF WIEMAR GERMANY

We can only understand the rise of Hitler in 1933 if we look at the atmosphere of crisis which prevailed in Germany under the Weimar Republic. One element in this crisis was political. The German nation had emerged relatively late as a major power in Europe. For centuries after England and France developed strong national states, Germany remained fragmented. Finally, Bismark united the various German states in 1870. As if to make up for lost time, the new nation quickly developed into one of the major economic, political and military powers of Europe. In 1918, however, Germany experienced the first of a series of blows.

After four years of intense and exhausting effort, Germany lost the First World War. The four major powers on the winning side, England, France, Italy and the United States, then handed Germany a harsh peace treaty. The Versailles Treaty was at odds with the gentle spirit of Woodrow Wilson's Fourteen Points; and what made matters worse, Germany had developed a democratic form of government, the Weimar Republic, at least partly in anticipation of earning a generous peace settlement. The sequence of events in 1918-1919 produced a sense of humiliation, frustration and bitterness in Germany. Coinciding as it did with Germany's first attempt at democracy, it won few friends for a democratic system.[4]

Germany also experienced a serious economic crisis, or series of crises, during the Weimar period. The normal trauma of postwar economic adjustment was exacerbated for Germany by an Allied demand for reparation payments. Based on the assumption that Germany was responsible for the war, an assumption not shared by Germans,[5] Germany was made to pay. One result was a period of hyperinflation in

1922, during which literally trillions of marks were required to buy a loaf of bread. A few years after this crisis was resolved, the worldwide Great Depression hit. The German economy suffered increasing rates of poverty and unemployment from 1930 to 1933, so that a genuine panic atmosphere prevailed. Without this crisis, Hitler probably would not have come to power.

During the 1920s, Germany also experienced a social crisis caused by the rapid pace of industrialization and urbanization. The industrial revolution struck Germany later than it did England or the United States, and problems associated with industrialization -- urban crime, prostitution, changing moral values, reduced church attendance, class division -- arrived with an upsetting suddenness in the already troubled 1920's. This was also a period of mobility and increasing democracy, so that Germany suddenly faced a pluralistic society, one in which Jews, socialists, union leaders and other "outsiders" gained legal rights and visibility.

33

Finally, Germany experienced a cultural crisis in the 1920s. All of the changes outlined above occurred in an open, democratic society which encouraged cultural and artistic experimentation and change; Berlin became a world cultural center during this era. But almost all of the cultural developments, from Bauhaus architecture to atonal music and avant garde art, were challenging to traditional values. Many a middle class Lutheran condemned these developments as frivolous, immoral, decadent and un-German.[6]

In the midst of this crisis atmosphere of the Weimar Republic, some groups welcomed the changes -- chiefly, those whose rights had earlier been repressed. The Protestant churches, however, had enjoyed the good old days. The church had been closely tied to the small states of local princes and the Hohenzollern emperors, and had prospered also in the traditional, rural areas and among the respectable middle classes. Modernization and industrialization, however, resulted in less respect for church leaders and fewer people in the pews. The church was also opposed to political parties which advocated liberalization, especially socialists or Marxists, because they were usually anti-clerical or even atheistic as well.

One political party during the Weimar period, the German National People's Party (DNVP), combined the nationalism and Christian values most congenial to German Protestants.[7] This rightwing party was anti-democratic, anti-Weimar, and longed for a return to an authoritarian state. In the early 1930s, however, the DNVP was outmaneuvered by a more popular rightwing group, the National Socialist or Nazi Party (NSDAP). Large numbers of Christians had not supported Hitler before he came to power in 1933. His background and political style were considered vulgar by traditional conservatives. Nazi Stormtroopers (SA) committed acts of violence in the streets, and some Nazi theoreticians preached a racist, biological antisemitism that was unacceptable to most Christians (who regarded their own version of antisemitism as more spiritual and refined). Hitler preached an authoritarian society and a return to past values, including family and traditional German culture. When he became the only viable rightwing alternative, about 80% of the Protestant clergy, those who were anti-Weimar, welcomed him more-or-less enthusiastically.[8] The only main exception were those pastors or theologians, such as Paul Tillich or Karl Barth, who were politically leftist or even religious socialists in their orientation.

The political, economic, social and cultural crises in Weimar Germany help explain Protestant support for Hitler. They do not, however, explain the Barmen Declaration. We must consider another background element, the long-simmering problem of Protestant disunity in Germany. Since the time of Martin Luther, the Protestant church in Germany had suffered from a problem of disunity. First, the Reformation produced two main branches of Protestants, Lutheran and Reformed. Secondly, the political fragmentation of Germany resulted in a church fragmentation as well. Each separate German state had its own state church, so that even by the twentieth century more than two dozen independent state churches (Landeskirchen) existed.

The denominational and regional divisions of German Protestantism had long been recognized as something of an embarrassment; efforts toward reunification dated back at least to the early nineteenth century. During the Napoleonic wars, German nationalists such as Fichte, Arndt and Jahn called for national unity; they also called for a unified Protestant church. Frederick William III of Prussia managed to create the Prussian Union, a church combining Lutheran and Reformed, in time to celebrate the three hundredth anniversary of the Reformation in 1817. Several smaller states followed suit in the next few years; but this movement had several limitations and it was neither taken up by the majority of German states nor even considered at the national level. Lutheran and Reformed churches were left continuing separate identities under the umbrella of the Union. Even with these compromises, vigorous opposition was aroused among confessional Lutherans, some of whom ultimately split off as the Evangelical Lutheran Church in Prussia.

German nationalism grew as part of the abortive revolutions of 1848. Church leaders responded by organizing several national church conferences, such as the Wittenburg Conference of 1848. These conferences provided a vehicle for communication and some cooperation between the various churches for the next fifty years. But even with the unification of Germany under Bismark, no unified national church (Reichskirche) could be achieved. In 1901, Kaiser Wilhelm II expressed his hope for a unified Protestant church in his lifetime; two years later a German Evangelical Church League (Deutsche Evangelische Kirchenbund) was established, with the cooperation of twenty-eight Protestant state churches.[9] But this remained an umbrella organization rather than a national church; each state church retained its autonomy.

Despite a century of increasing cooperation among German Protestant churches, unification had lagged behind the

political unification of the country. In
1933, at a time when enthusiasm for national
unity was an overwhelming part of the Nazi
appeal, the problem of church disunity
seemed awkward or even unpatriotic. But the
church faced a second major problem in its
theological division.

N   Theological division is at least as old
as Christianity and hardly unique to
Germany. However, the splintering effects of
Luther's Reformation had provoked an acute
and divisive style of German leadership in
theological developments. One particular
theologian, Karl Barth, one of the most
important theologians of this century,
played a major role as author of the Barmen
Declaration. Therefore, we will attempt to
see Barth's theology in this historical
perspective.

By the nineteenth century three major
strands could be identified in German
Protestant theology; (1) Orthodoxy was
rooted in the institutional church and
stressed correct belief based upon the
Lutheran or Reformed confessions. (2) As
early as the seventeenth century, a pietist

movement had insisted that genuine faith is more important than correctness of belief, or conversely, that one could know and understand correct doctrine without experiencing personal conviction. Pietists therefore stressed personal faith, prayer, Bible study, and a loving community of born-again Christians, in contrast to the formal, doctrinal, orthodox churches. (3) Finally, the Enlightenment and its stress upon rationalism had led to a scholarly strand known as liberal theology.

Liberal theology dominated the theological faculties of German universities in the nineteenth century. Based on the assumption that the message of God to humanity can be understood in its purest form through careful, rational, scholarly inquiry, these theologians applied their best academic tools -- historical, literary and linguistic -- in a massive quest for the pure Christian message. The fruit of their scholarship has become a staple of modern theology; German scholarship has provided us with an improved understanding of the world and of the Bible. But by the turn of the century, a nagging suspicion developed that liberal theology might not adequately express Christian faith. The search for a historical Jesus, for example, began with high hopes and was largely frustrated. Relativism was a serious problem for all historians by the end of the nineteenth century, leaving scholars unable to find the certain truths for which they searched.

Soren Kierkegaard, a nineteenth-century Danish philisopher, provided a way out of this imbroglio for twentieth-century theologians of the "dialectical" school. In the 1920s, Karl Barth became the premier representative of this new viewpoint, arguing that liberal theology was based on the wrong assumptions and asked the wrong questions. Borrowing from Kierkegaard, Barth stressd the "infinite qualitative distinction" between God and humanity. Because of this infinite gap, a human being cannot presume to understand God or approach God through reason. Barth rejected all attempts to approach God with the pejorative label "religion." In contrast to religion, Christianity is the recognition that God comes to humans, God is self-revealing, and that a human is thus given the opportunity

to accept God's message. Barth was a
trained theologian who employed the tools of
liberal scholarship, but his Christian faith
was preeminent. He began with Kierkegaard's
"leap of faith," and from that position of
faith in the basic postulates of
Christianity he built his theological
analysis. Barth's "dialectical" or
"neo-orthodox" theology rang across Germany
like a church bell in the 1920s. Not
everyone accepted it, of course; but many
twentieth-century theologians now begin with
the presupposition of a leap of faith
instead of the nineteenth-century
presupposition that reason and scholarship
can identify God's message.

Barth's theology was sometimes called
"crisis" theology, because he perceived the
crisis between God and humans that only
God's grace can overcome. But the term
"crisis theology" also resonates with the
situation in Germany in the 1920s.
Theologians in that era faced the
specifically theological crisis of the
apparent demise of liberal theology, and
they were also part of the much larger
crisis being described here. We can now see

that because of this multifaceted crisis, the German Protestant churches were not in a position to make the critical decisions required of them in 1933. They were largely anti-democratic, anti-modern and nationalistic in their political and social outlook; they practically equated Christian culture with the traditional German culture. They were divided denominationally and geographically, and they were in a state of theological flux when Adolf Hitler came to power on January 30, 1933.

THE EVENTS OF 1933 AND 1934

The "German Christians" were a small and relatively obscure group of Protestants when Hitler came to power, but they suddenly found themselves in a position of unprecedented power. Tying themselves to the coattails of the Nazi Party, they nearly formed and controlled a unified, national Protestant church. They failed in the end for a variety of reasons, not the least because they were much less important to Hitler than he was to them. But during 1933 and 1934, they held center stage in church affairs.

The first German Christian group was
formed in Thuringia by Julius Leutheuser
and Seigfried Leffler. As early as 1924,
they formed an association of National
Socialist pastors with the twin goals of
evangelism and opposition to communists and
free thinkers. By 1927, their political
activities caused their ouster from the
clergy; but they persisted in their attempts
to combine National Socialism and
Christianity, syncretizing the "Church
Movement of German Christians"
(Kirchenbewegung Deutsche Christen) in 1929.

A second group of Nazi clergy developed
a German Christian movement in Berlin.
Jurgen Hossenfelder organized this group
early in 1932 as the National Socialist
Pastors' League. In June it became the
"Faith Movement of German Christians"
(Glaubensbewegung Deutsche Christen), and
published its list of goals. These included
an endorsement of the Aryan race and the
German nation and a Protestant church built
upon this foundation. In the spirit of
national unity now represented by the Nazi
Party, Protestants should create a united

"Volkskirche" (people's church) to replace
the divided churches of the past. The
confessional basis would be vague.

> We confess a positive Christian
> faith, corresponding to the German
> spirit of Luther and heroic
> piety.[11]

They lamented the historical failure of
the German church.

> In the fateful struggle
> over German freedom and the
> German future, the church and its
> leadership has proven itself too
> weak. Up until now the church has
> contributed nothing in the
> decisive struggle against
> atheistic Marxism and the
> spiritually alien Center Party (a
> Roman Catholic political
> party).[12]

The proposed national church should
fight for the purity of the German race,
protect it from the unfit and inferior, and

oppose any connection with Jews, including a Jewish mission or mixed marriage.[13]

In the Prussian church elections of November, 1932, Hossenfelder's German Christians received one-third of the votes. This does not represent overwhelming support for the German Christians, but it gave them a strong foothold in the strongest and most important of the regional churches even before Hitler came to power. In early 1933, they attempted to build upon this foundation.

On March 5, 1933, Hitler held a national election in an attempt to curry a mandate for his policies. He succeeded only partially however, despite heavy-handed tactics against his political opponents; he received forty-four percent of the vote, which allowed him to build a majority government, but with the help of other rightwing parties. Then, apparently, Hitler decided to make an appeal for church support in an attempt to broaden his political base. On March 23, he made a conciliatory speech in which he promised to respect the existing treaties between the regional churches and their state governments, and he described Christianity as the fundamental moral basis of the German people.[14] Lingering doubts among German Protestant leaders whether Hitler were a proper leader of the German renewal began to fade and expressions of support increased.

During March, the German Christians also intensified their demands for a national church. In order to avoid losing control of the situation, leaders of the German Evangelical Church League (DEK) appointed a three-man committee to write a new church constitution. On April 23, H. Kapler, head of the DEK; A. Marahrens, Bishop of Hanover; and H.A. Hesse, a Reformed pastor in Elberfeld, began their deliberations. Two days later, Hitler intervened in the process, at least indirectly, by appointing a German Christian, Ludwig Müller, as his personally authorized representative for church affairs. Müller was then added to the group, and the foursome produced a constitution for a unified national church on May 26.

While this constitution was being written it became apparent that selection of a national bishop would prove a major test of German Christian strength. The German Christians argued during May that Ludwig Müller, since he possessed the confidence of the Führer, was the only logical choice. Müller, however, was unacceptable to broad elements within the church. First of all, his lack of national stature was an impediment; clearly he was only being considered because of his preferment by Hitler. Secondly, the German Christians were considered to be a small, radical group who mixed politics indiscriminately with religion. Therefore, a group calling themselves the "Young Reformation Movement" (Jungreformatorische Bewegung) under the leadership of Walther Künneth, Hans Lilje and Martin Niemöller, proposed an alternative to the German Christian direction. They proclaimed their "joyful Yes to the new German state," but insisted the church must "fulfill its assignment from God in full freedom from political influence."[15] As a candidate for national bishop they proposed Freidrich von

Bodelschwingh, the widely respected director
of a hospital at Bethel.

How or when a national bishop could be
legally selected was not clear, but the
campaigns launched for Müller and
Bodelschwingh forced the hand of
representatives of the state churches.
Meeting on May 26-27. They selected
Bodelschwingh; he attempted to take office.
Over the next month, however,
Bodelschwingh's position became untenable.
Ironically, for a group which was
philosophically anti-democratic, the German
Christians protested that Bodelschwingh had
not been elected by a democratic vote of
church members. In the midst of a flurry of
backbiting and positioning, a critical
change took place in the Prussian church.
The moderate leader, Kapler, stepped down as
president of the Prussian Church Council on
June 21, and the cultural minister of
Prussia appointed a political commissar for
church affairs, August Jäger, on June 24.
Jäger immediately removed moderates in the
Prussian church administration and replaced
them with German Christians. Bodelschwingh,
recognizing that these events undercut his

authority and that they would not be
effectively opposed by the DEK, submitted
his resignation that same day, June 24. On
June 28 Ludwig Müller occupied the offices
of the DEK in Berlin with Stormtrooper
support. He declared that in view of the
crisis, he would take over emergency
leadership of the DEK. A new committee was
appointed, a new constitution for a national
church written, and on July 11 this
constitution received unanimous approval of
the state churches.

The next step involved church
elections, in which a German Christian slate
of candidates ran against a slate known as
"Gospel and Church" put up by the Young
Reformation Movement. The day before the
elections, Hitler made a surprise speech in
support of the German Christian slate. On
July 23, with large numbers of brown-shirted
members packing the pews, the German
Christians won 60-80% of the vote. The
Young Reformers controlled the churches only
in Bavaria and Westphalia. On September 27,
the newly elected National Synod selected
Müller as national bishop, officially

completing the process by which the German Christians took over the new church.

In the midst of apparent victory for the German Christians, however, the seeds of defeat had already been sown. Suspicions regarding both the stature and the theological acceptability of German Christian leaders had already existed. Now the blatant political interference in church affairs aroused concern among large numbers of Protestant clergy and laity who were otherwise quite pleased with the Hitler regime. And a series of events in Prussia, where the German Christians were most firmly in control, accelerated the dissatisfaction.

On September 5-6, 1933, a newly elected synod of the Prussian church met. It was soon to be known as the "Brown Synod" due to the dominance of German Christians. First, the structure of the Prussian church was changed in order to get rid of moderate officials within the church bueaucracy and replace them with German Christians. Then, two restrictions were placed on clergy within the Prussian church, one requiring "political reliability" and another imposing

the "Aryan Paragraph." Karl Koch, president
of the Westphalian synod, protested these
actions, but was shouted down. At that
point, he and Martin Niemöller led a
walkout of the "Gospel and Church" group.
Two weeks later, on September 21, Niemöller
invited participation in a "Pastor's
Emergency League," a group opposed to German
Christian policies. By January, more than
7,000 members had joined, about half the
active Protestant pastors in Germany. This
was the beginning of active opposition to
German Christian church government.

German Christians escalated the
conflict one stage higher in November, 1933.
Eager to celebrate the Reformation in style
on this 450th anniversary of Martin Luther's
birth, they organized a rally for November
13 in the Berlin Sports Palace. Twenty
thousand attended the rally and thus became
witnesses to a major German Christian
tactical mistake. Dr. R. Krause, a regional
German Christian leader in Berlin,
enthusiastically outlined future goals,
including removal from the Christian
tradition of all traces of its Jewish past.
Arguing that Christianity was in reality a

strong Aryan religion, he advocated removal of the Jewish Old Testament from the Bible, removal of the "Rabbi" Paul's influence, and change of emphasis from the crucified to the heroic Jesus as model.

The Sports Palace rally caused a scandal. Krause was quickly fired from his position in the German Christian movement, but the damages could not be contained. On December 6, Ludwig Müller disassociated himself from the German Christian group by resigning his leadership position in the movement; and on December 21, Hossenfelder resigned as national leader. Müller remained powerful as national bishop and the German Christian ideology was not yet broken, but the omminous victory of the German Christians was badly undercut by the end of 1933.

January, 1934, produced another dramatic turnaround in the church struggle, but this one was to the advantage of Müller. On January 25, Hitler received five representatives of the opposition movement within the church. These men, Bishops Marahrens, Meiser and Wurm,

President Koch of Westphalia, and Niemöller representing the Pastors' Emergency League, intended to demand Müller's resignation as national bishop. To their surprise, Hitler counterpunched by reading the transcript of a telephone conversation between Niemöller and one of his colleagues, Künneth. Niemöller had discussed the possibility of bringing pressure on Hitler through the aged president of Germany, von Hindenburg. This discretion, which Hitler picked up by tapping Niemöller's telephone, devastated the delegation. Müller then met with church leaders over the next two days, pulling back from the apparent radicalism of his earlier stance, and receiving a statement of support from the very church leaders who had hoped for his resignation two days earlier. Niemöller's effectiveness and the previously solid support for his Pastor's Emergency League quickly began to dissipate. Niemöller himself was removed from his pastorate on March 1, 1934, found deficient in terms of the Prussian "political reliability clause."

Despite the apparent setback for Niemöller and the opposition movement, another development in the first six months of 1934 kept the Church Struggle alive. A twofold thrust led toward a separate Confessing Church outside the official national church and a statement of faith in opposition to German Christian heresy.

On January 3-4, 1934, a Free Reformed Synod met in Barmen, accepting for itself a statement by Karl Barth, "A Declaration on the correct understanding of the Reformation confessions in the German Evangelical Church of the present." This statement was also approved February 18-19 by a Free Protestant Synod in the Rhineland. In March, police dissolved the Westphalian Synod; but it promptly reformed under Karl Koch as the Westphalian Confessing Synod and approved Barth's January statement. In March, three of the most powerful Lutheran churches also moved in the direction of rebellion against the official national church. On March 13, Bishops Meiser of Bavaria and Wurm of Württemberg had a personal visit with Hitler in which they withdrew their January 27 declaration of loyalty to Müller. The Bavarian church then convoked a "Nuremberg Council," which helped prepare for the

Barmen Synod.   Also in March, Bishop
Marahrens of Hannover came under attack from
the national church.   Müller hoped to force
the Hannoverian church to give up its
autonomy and its bishop, and become an
integral part of the national church.   But
Marahrens fought back, won the support of
his clergy and membership in a vote of
confidence, and retained the autonomy of his
church.   A similar attempt in April to
unseat Bishop Wurm of Württemberg also
failed, leading to the formation in Ulm on
April 22 of a Confessing Church as the
"legal Protestant Church of Germany."

All of these actions were inherently
rebellious.   They denied the authority of
the national church under Müller's
leadership and proclaimed the need for a
national church established without
political interference and based upon an
acceptable theology.   By May, 1934, the
logic of this situation led to plans for the
first Synod of the Confessing Church at
Barmen.   In preparation for this synod, a
three-person committee, led by Karl Barth, met
in mid-May to draft a declaration of the
basic principles for a German Protestant

church. This document, approved at the
Barmen Synod, May 29-31, 1934, became known
as the Barmen Declaration. It is the
fundamental document on which the Confessing
Church built its opposition to Ludwig
Müller, the official national church
structure, and the German Christian
ideology.

The Barmen Declaration received fairly
widespread support and became the
"confession" of the Confessing Church. In
October, 1934, Müller and his henchman,
August Jäger, made one last attempt to
break the Bavarian and Württemberg churches
by placing Bishops Meiser and Wurm under
house arrest and forcing integration of
these two churches into the national church
structure. But massive popular oppostion in
Bavaria and Württemberg forced Müller to
give up on this plan. The Confessing Church
then convened its second national synod at
Dahlem in response to this new crisis. On
October 19-20, it declared itself the
legitimate national church, arguing that
Müller's violation of the church
constitution had disqualified his claim to

lead a legally constituted church government.

In late October, Hitler resolved this newest church crisis by finally giving up on Müller. He invited Marahrens, Meiser and Wurm to Berlin on October 26. Four days later he met with them and reestablished their authority as bishops of their respective churches. Jäger was fired and although Müller did not resign, his power was broken. After eighteen months, Hitler had decided that his attempt to play church politics on the side of the German Christians was a failure. Apparently the Confessing Church had at least caused an ecclesiastical stalemate.[16]

Despite appearances in October, 1934, the Confessing Church had overcome only its weakest enemy, Ludwig Müller and the German Christians. The Nazi state continued to harass individual Confessing Church leaders, especially Niemöller and Bonhöffer. Through its cultural ministry and influence over university theological faculties it successfully undercut Confessing Church activities over the next few years. The

Confessing Church itself became divided
between the so-called "radical" wing under
Niemöller and the "intact" Lutheran
churches of Hannover, Bavaria, and
Württemberg. When these three churches
reestableshed their autonomy vis-à-vis
Müller, they became suspicious of their
Confessing Church allies. Had the Barmen
declaration been too infuenced by Barth's
Reformed background? Was the
Niemöller-Bonhöffer wing possibly
unpatriotic or even treasonous? The first
two years proved the best years for the
Confessing Church. Issues were clearcut and
the villains visible. The next ten years --
with Barth in Switzerland, Niemöller in
prison, and Bonhöffer and others hounded by
the Gestapo -- proved less glorious.
Punctuated by occasional acts of bravery,
the Protestant church as a whole failed to
oppose or condemn the increasingly brutal
policies of the Nazi regime against its own
citizens and neighbors.

THE BARMEN DECLARATION

     The Barmen Synod produced several
statements and resolutions.[17] The first

of these serves as an introduction to the
main Barmen Declaration, clarifying the
purpose and intentions of the Synod:

The Confessional Synod of the
German Evangelical Church met in
Barmen, May 29-31, 1934....In
fidelity to their Confession of
Faith, members of Lutheran,
Reformed, and United Churches
sought a common message for the
need and temptation of the Church
in our day. With gratitude to God
they were convinced that they have
been given a common word to utter.
It was not their intention to
found a new Church or to form a
union. For nothing was farther
from their minds than the
abolition of the confessional
status of our Churches. Their
intention was, rather, to
withstand in faith and unanimity
the destruction of the Confession
of Faith, and thus of the
Evangelical Church in Germany. In
opposition to attempts to
establish the unity of the German

Evangelical Church by means of
false doctrine, by the use of
force and insincere practices, the
Confessional Synod insists that
the unity of the Evangelical
churches in Germany can come only
from the Word of God in faith
through the Holy Spirit. Thus
alone is the Church renewed.[18]

Although German Christians are not mentioned
by name, the "temptation" to be withstood by
the church is clearly the one to which the
German Christians had succumbed. Their
combined enthusiasm for the Nazi state and
for church unity had overcome all other
considerations, leading them to "false
doctrine," "force," and "insincere
practices" as means to establish a national
church administration.

This statement appeals to individual
Protestant congregations in Germany for
support of the Barmen Synod's position. In
doing so, it reassures those congregations
that the question is one of church politics,
not national politics. The Barmen
Declaration is not an attack on the Nazi

state: "Be not deceived by loose talk, as
if we meant to oppose the unity of the
German nation!" Congregations and
individuals are then encouraged to evaluate
the statements of Barmen in the light of
Scripture.

The Barmen Declaration itself,
officially called the "Theological
Declaration Concerning the Present Situation
of the German Evangelical Church," builds
upon the constitution of the German
Evangelical Church as written and approved
in July, 1933. The preamble to this
document quotes first from Article 1 of the
constitution:

> The inviolable foundation of the
> German Evangelical Church is the
> gospel of Jesus Christ as it is
> attested for us in Holy Scripture
> and brought to light again in the
> Confessions of the Reformation.
> The full powers that the Church
> needs for its mission are hereby
> determined and limited.

Then it quotes from Article 2: "The German Evangelical Church is divided into member Churches (Landeskirchen)." These two statements are the basis upon which Barmen disputes the legality of the German Christian administration of the German Evangelical Church. By not restricting itself to the gospel and by attacking the existence of individual Landeskirchen, it had violated its own constitutions. The preamble then draws this conclusion:

> We are bound together by the confession of the one lord of the one, holy, catholic, and apostolic Church.
>
> We publicly declare before all Evangelical Churches in Germany that what they hold in common in this Confession is grievously imperiled, and with it the unity of the German Evangelical Church. It is threatened by the teaching methods and actions of the ruling Church party of the "German Christians" and of the Church administration carried on by them. These have

become more and more apparent
during the first year of the
existence of the German
Evangelical Church. This threat
consists in the fact that the
theological basis, in which the
German Evangelical Church is
united, has been continually and
systematically thwarted and
rendered ineffective by alien
principles, on the part of the
leaders and spokesmen of the
"German Christians" as well as on
the part of the Church
administration. When these
principles are held to be valid,
then, according to all the
Confessions in force among us, the
Church ceases to be the Church,
and the German Evangelical Church,
as a federation of Confessional
Churches, becomes intrinsically
impossible.

The main body of the Barmen Declaration
consists of six theses, which are declared
"the indispensable theological basis of the
German Evangelical Church." The first

concerns revelation. German Christians had professed to see God's revelation in the rise of Hitler and the National Socialist state. This new message justified such transmutations of traditional church doctrine as removing Judaism from the Judeo-Christian tradition. In opposition to this line of thought, the first Barmen thesis proclaims:

> Jesus Christ, as he is attested for us in Holy Scripture, is the one Word of God which we have to hear and which we have to trust and obey in life and in death.
>
> We reject the false doctrine, as though the Church could and would have to acknowledge as a source of its proclamation, apart from and besides this one Word of God, still other events and powers, figures and truths, as God's revelation.

German Christians also saw in the secular Nazi movement an exciting spiritual experience and spiritual community, which

they often compared unfavorably to the
comparatively dull and stodgy community of
the church.   The second Barmen thesis
responds with an affirmation of the totality
of God's claim upon the Christian:

> We reject the false doctrine,
> as though there were areas of our
> life in which we would not belong
> to Jesus Christ, but to other
> lords -- areas in which we would
> not need justification and
> sanctification through him.

The third thesis protests that the
Church should not allow the form of its
message or sacraments to sway with the
political wind.   The church's allegiance is
solely to Jesus Christ, "it is solely his
property."   Therefore,

> We reject the false doctrine, as
> though the Church were permitted to abandon
> the form of its message and order to its
> own pleasure or to changes in prevailing
> ideological and political convictions.

One of the forms of the institutional church involves its leadership structure. National Socialists represented and advocated the "Führerprinzip," the idea of strong, hierarchical, personal leadership, which they preferred to democracy. German Christians believed that the Nazi pattern of a Führer passing down decisions to obedient underlings should also prevail in the national church. The fourth Barmen thesis quotes Matthew 20:26, "whoever would be great among you must be your servant," and concludes,

> The various offices in the Church do not establish a dominion of some over others; on the contrary, they are for the exercise of the ministry entrusted to and enjoined upon the whole congregation.
>
> We reject the false doctrine, as though the Church, apart from this ministry, could and were permitted to give to itself, or allow to be given to it, special leaders vested with ruling powers.

The fifth Barmen thesis takes up the difficult question of church and state and their relationship to each other. It affirms that the state is a tool of God: "in the as yet unredeemed world in which the Church also exists, the State has by divine appointment the task of providing for justice and peace." Barth had amended the thesis to add,

> We reject the error, as though the State were the only and totalitarian order of human life. We reject the error, as though the Church had to conform to a particular form of the State in its message and form.

This statement, however, apparently implied to many participants at Barmen an attack upon the Nazi state, and an implicationcontrary to their actual sentiments. One of the important Lutheran representatives, Georg Merz, insisted the Synod should oppose German Christians, not the state. Averting an impasse, Barth rewrote this section and it was accepted as follows,

> We reject the false doctrine, as though the State, over and beyond its special commission, should and could become the single and totalitarian order of human life, thus fulfilling the Church's vocation as well.

> We reject the false doctrine, as though the Church, over and beyond its special commission, should and could appropriate the characteristics, the tasks, and the dignity of the State, thus itself becoming an organ of the State.[19]

The sixth Barmen thesis reaffirms a theme which recurs throughout the Declaration: the church must be autonomous, based upon its relationship to the Word of God in Christ.

> The Church's commission, upon which its freedom is founded, consists in delivering the message

of the free grace of God to all
people in Christ's stead, and
therefore in the ministry of his
own Word and work through sermon
and sacrament.

We reject the false doctrine,
as though the Church in human
arrogance could place the Word and
work of the Lord in the service of
any arbitrarily chosen desires,
purposes and plans.

After approving the above Declaration,
the Barmen Synod passed several additional
statements and resolutions. One of these,
"Declaration Concerning the Legal Status of
the German Evangelical Church," states the
argument by which the authority of Ludwig
Müller's Church administration is denied,

The unimpeachable basis of
the German Evangelical Church is
the gospel of Jesus Christ as it
is testified to in Holy Scripture
and brought to light again in the
confessions of the Reformation.
The present Reich Church
administration has abandoned this
unimpeachable basis and has been

guilty of numerous violations of
the law and the constitution. It
has thereby forfeited the claim to
be the legitimate administration
of the German Evangelical Church.

In place of Müller's administration, the
Barmen Synod proclaimed itself the
legitimate German Evangelical Church, and it
established an eleven-person Council of
Brethren to act as its working body.

We must now ask several questions
concerning the Barmen Declaration. Was it a
good theological statement? Was it a good
political statement? Does it have a message
for today?

Barth consciously molded the theology
of Barmen to attract the broadest possible
base of support against the German
Christians. It is not, therefore, a
complete confession of faith, for it does
not deal with controversial subjects such as
baptism or the meaning of the Eucharist.
Reformed and Lutheran Protestants could not
have agreed on these matters. Rather,
Barth isolated the single most objectionable

element in German Christian theology, the notion that God had now revealed a new message to humanity through German history. German Christians asserted that 1933 had been a religious year for Germans, that the German renewal under Hitler was of spiritual significance, and that Christians should be willing to change the outer forms of their Church structure and doctrinal understanding in order to tap fully this religious experience and make Christianity understandable and attractive to the average German. To Barth, this casual bending of Christian concepts and values represented the worst result of liberal theology, the idea that Christians could mold their understanding of the "essence" of Christianity according to their historical circumstances. The Barmen Declaration was thus a Christocentric, neo-orthodox statement that revelation comes only through Jesus Christ as presented to believers in the Bible, and it adds that the Church must be wholly free of political influence or interference to serve God properly.

We now see that the message of Hitler, valued so highly by the German Christians, was brutal and un-Christian. In contrast to the mistaken notions of the German Christians, the theological statements of Barmen appear to be unimpeachable truths. Nonetheless, the Barmen Declaration met with immediate criticism, not only from avowed German Christians but also from many others, especially conservative Lutherans from the three intact churches of Hannover, Württemberg and Bavaria. Two professors at Erlangen University, Werner Elert and Paul Althaus, quickly produced the "Ansbacher Ratschlag," an anti-Barmen statement representing the Erlangen theological faculty. Althaus later published an additional statement taking issue with the theology of Barmen. Even Hermann Sasse, another of the staunch Lutherans at Erlangen, questioned Barmen. Despite the fact that Sasse was an early opponent of the German Christians and an approving participant at the Barmen Synod, he penned his reservations about the document almost at the same time he cast his supporting vote.

What were the main objections? Althaus and Elert viewed Barmen, first of all, as a

slap at the German renewal under National
Socialism. Their enthusiasm for this new
state, coupled with their deep   concern
that the fragile spirit of unity not be
broken, resulted in a desire to muffle all
criticism. Although they too criticized
German Christians, they insisted that
references to the new state be explicit and
glowing, as seen in the "Ansbacher
Ratschlag:"

> As Christians we honor with thanks
> toward God...every authority...as
> a tool of divine preservation....
> In this knowledge we as believing
> Christians thank God that he has
> given to our people in its time of
> need the <u>Führer</u> as a "pious and
> faithful leader" and the National
> Socialist political system as
> "good government," a government
> with "decency and honor."[20]

Though we realize how wrong this view of
Hitler was, it shows us how much patriotic
Germans rejected the Barmen denial of a rela-
tion between God and the State--especially
Lutherans, who inherited Martin   Luther's

strong interpretation of Romans 13 on obedience to state authority.

A second problem emerged for Lutherans, the concern that Barmen was secretly an attempt to produce a united church based upon a new confession of faith. In planning for the Barmen Synod, Barth and his Reformed colleagues showed their cognizance of this fear and insisted the Declaration not be considered a confession of faith. The Synod explicitly stated this and expressed its respect for the individual confessions of member churches. But Hermann Sasse, after voting for the Barmen Declaration, immediately wrote a statement revealing the touchiness of this issue for some Lutherans. First, he acknowledges his approval of the six theses of Barmen, "although I am of the opinion that the text here and there can be interpreted differently by Lutheran theologians than by theologians of the Reformed confession."[21] He then asserts that the Barmen Synod as a group cannot establish true or false doctrine. That can only be done by a Lutheran Synod for Lutheran or a Reformed Synod for Reformed. Therefore, the conclusions of the Synod, "whether they are true or false in content, can never lay claim to being obligatory."[22] Many Lutherans shared Sasse's concern for confessional purity. For them, the Barmen Declaration was first suspect because written by Barth, a Reformed theologian. Secondly, the very nature of Barmen as a common statement triggered a fear that it glossed over confessional differences too carelessly.

A third form of critique attacked the theological substance of individual Barmen theses. Paul Althaus, for example, attacked the first Barmen thesis for expressing too narrow and Christological an interpretation of God's revelation. He agreed that God's primary revelation to human beings comes in Christ through the Bible, and he opposed the German Christians for exaggerating the significance of 1933. But he argued that God can and does reveal himself to humanity through historical events, even though this secondary form of revelation can be understood properly only in light of the primary revelation of Christ.[23] Is Barth's view of revelation too narrow? Certainly the God of the Old Testament

revealed himself through history. Many
Christians have continued to look for God's
hand in historical events. Therefore, the
first Barmen thesis might produce a
theological debate today. Barth's narrow
view of revelation addressed the
circumstances of 1933-1934, however, more
effectively than did Althaus' broader one.

Althaus also criticized Barmen three.
He argues, with justice, that the rituals of
the Christian church and forms of the
Christian message have often adjusted to
historical events and circumstances in the
past. For example, the Pope in Rome
emulated the administrative style of Roman
emperors, and the early church gave
Christian content to pagan customs and
festivals. Althaus asserted that the
outward forms of the Christian church should
once again bend with the times, thereby
presenting a more attractive and relevant
face to the German Volk.[24] Althaus'
message was ironically presupposed in the
1920s by Paul Tillich and other religious
socialists. They reformulated the Christian
message with a leftist slant to appeal to
the working classes at that time, but later

condemned reformulations appealing to Nazis on the right. The Christians church has also witnessed manifestations of this theme since 1945, from guitar-accompanied liturgies to liberation theology. Perhaps a distinction can be made between the church "abandoning" the form of its message (the wording of Barmen three) and only "bending" the forms. It might also be possible to distinguish between "prevailing ideological and political convictions" which are amenable to Christianity and those which are inimicable, but Christians in Nazi Germany did not make that distinction very successfully. The third Barmen thesis was a useful statement for its time and place; it too would provoke an argument today.

Was the Barmen Declaration a good political statement? Here the obvious yes must be qualified. Barmen did oppose German Christian control of the German Evangelical Church and Nazi interference in the affairs of the Church. But it is now apparent the politics of Barmen did not go far enough. One must state categorically that the Barmen Declaration did not oppose National Socialism itself nor Adolf Hitler himself.

It opposed, rather, the deification of National Socialism and political interference in church affairs. Although some supporters of Barmen, among them Bonhöffer, attacked both German Christians and National Socialism, the Barmen Declaration very carefully avoided this stance. Therefore, many Confessing Church members were able to preface attacks upon Müller or statements supportive of Barmen with professions of appreciation for the German rebirth and loyalty to the Nazi state.

The Aryan Paragraph issue provides an example of the political inadequacy of the Barmen Declaration. The Prussian "Brown Synod" of September, 1933, voted to apply the Aryan Paragraph to clergy and officials of the church: persons of Jewish origin would be removed from the Christian clergy, unless they had served prior to 1914 or had been front line soldiers during World War I (concessions made earlier to President Hindenburg when the Nazis applied the Aryan concept to civil servants). About twenty-nine of the 18,000 Protestant church officials in Germany were of Jewish origin, and eleven of these met one of the two exemption requirements.[25] Despite these small numbers, Rudolf Bultmann and the Marburg theological faculty quickly published a Gutachten attacking the Aryan Paragraph as un-Christian.[26] Many reputable theologians, however, including Paul Althaus, Emanuel Hirsch and Gerhard Kittel, prepared statements at least partially endorsing the concept. It was common for them to begin by asserting oneness in Christ and the efficacy of baptism for people of Jewish origins. Each, however, acknowledged the significance of the Jewish problem for Germany, accepting many of the cultural and racial stereotypes about Jews as a danger to the German nation. On that basis they acknowledged the right of the state to request Jews to hold back from significant positions in German society, including that of the Protestant clergy.[27] Paul Althaus noted that other qualifications, such as gender and age, had traditionally been applied to the clergy and he argued that race might legitimately be added to the list. Althaus typically counseled moderation in actually removing Jewish-Christian clergy, preferring a policy

of attrition to one of ouster.[28] But each
of these three men shared a perspective of
anti-semitic prejudice in acknowledging a
"Jewish question" at all, each strove to
support rather than oppose Nazi policies,
and each was willing to read the Barmen
concept of oneness in Christ in line with
these beliefs.

As early as April, 1933, Dietrich
Bonhöffer delivered a public lecture
asserting that the "Jewish question" and
Nazi ill treatment of Jews was a matter of
Christian concern.[29] Bonhöffer was one
of the very few who constantly pressed this
theme, and he hoped that the Confessing
Church would take a stand. But the Church
never met his expectations on this issue,
although on one occasion in 1936, the
Confessing Church did issue a statement
intended for Hitler:

> If the Christian within the scope of
> the National Socialist worldview is
> forced to an antisemitism which
> requires hatred of Jews, the Christian
> commandment to love one's neighbor
> stands for him as a contrary law.[30]

There were also individual acts of kindness toward Jews, some of them very brave. But love, concern, and assistance for Jews never fundamentally marked the behavior or policies of the Confessing Church.

The career of Gerhard Kittel raises the "Jewish question" to a higher level of concern. Prior to 1933, Kittel established himself as an authority on Judaism at the time of Christ and its relation to the early Christian faith. Kittel enjoyed an international reputation as editor of the Theological Dictionary of the New Testament, a standard reference work. But between 1933 and 1945, Kittel parlayed his expertise in Jewish history and theology into an important position in the major Nazi research institute on the "Jewish question." In the process, Kittel argued for Christian support of harsh anti-Jewish measures. He insisted that God does not require Christians to be soft and sentimental, but to face harsh truths and act accordingly. Kittel also devoted his research activities to describing the moral, intellectual, spiritual, and racial depravity of Jews.

When he was arrested by the Allies in 1945, Kittel, who had been the pride of the Tübingen theological faculty, defended his position in the Nazi Party and research institute as well-meaning attempts to fight the materialistic, biological antisemitism of radical Nazis with the spiritual antisemitism of a Christian. He continued to insist that his hatred of the modern Jew was consistent with the antisemitism of Jesus and Paul.[31]

In the face of Gerhard Kittel's attack on the Jews and many other Christian attacks, some more extreme than his, it is unfortunate that the Confessing Church did not address this problem persistently and forthrightly, condemning Nazi Jewish policies as un-Christian. The Confessing Church also failed to focus on other crimes of the Nazi state: arrest without warrant, imprisonment without trial, intimidation and violence administered by state and party officials. Germany invaded Poland in 1939 and precipitated the Second World War, an act condemned at the time outside Germany and subsequently deemed a war crime by the Nuremberg Tribunal. Christians in Germany

almost universally supported the war effort,
at least as revealed in public statements
and sermons. Under these circumstances, the
politics of the Barmen Declaration now
appear to have been too indirect and too
tame.

Does the Barmen Declaration have a
message for today? Some Christians in
postwar Germany have interpreted Barmen to
mean that Christians should never take sides
politically, that they should stick to
preaching the gospel only. These are
generally social conservatives who did not
want to see the church opposing South
African racism, taking part in
Latin-American liberation theological
action, or involving itself in the peace
movement. Clearly Barmen was telling German
Christians that <u>their</u> political views
might not be seen as having religious,
revelatory significance. But Barth himself
became politically active in his opposition
to the Nazi regime, assuming God was on his
side. And Martin Niemöller became actively
involved in the peace movement in Germany
after 1945. Apolitical behavior does not

seem to have been the lesson of Barmen for the "radical" leaders of Barmen.

This theme receives further support from the life of Dietrich Bonhöffer. With hindsight we now see that the Church in Germany failed to recognize the extreme forms of political injustice in Nazi Germany which have since invited nearly universal condemnation of that regime. Bonhöffer, on the other hand, did oppose Nazism, even to the point of wishing Germany's defeat in war and actively working to assassinate Hitler. He thereby emerges for most Americans and many Germans as the hero. If we judge Bonhöffer rightly, and I think we do, then the final lesson of Barmen is this: the Christian faith requires an intense commitment to acting upon political, social and moral issues in the light of the Gospel.

Christians in Germany were blind to much that is now obvious to us. In their conservatism, nationalism, and racism, they were anti-democratic and jingoistic, assuming that their fight for culture was also the fight for Christian existence. Going beyond Barmen, Bonhöffer encouraged them to throw off their nationalistic and conservative blinders and learn to live as Christians in "a world come of age." If Barmen has a message for us today, it is that we develop a Christian vision beyond the blindspots of our time and place.

CONCLUSION

The Barmen Declaration is a good statement. It took the right stance at the right time on an important issue, and it did so in a manner calculated to win broad support. Theologically, the Barmen Declaration is sound, if not entirely beyond dispute. Politically, Barmen and the Confessing Church failed by not going far enough. They protected their own domain, the autonomy of the church; but they did not defend their weaker neighbors nor attack the evil of the Nazi regime. Only a few individuals did that.

It may not be appropriate for us to condemn Christians in Nazi Germany. They faced extremely difficult decisions in extremely difficult circumstances. But it is appropriate for us to recognize the weaknesses, divisions and failures in the response of Confessing Christians in Germany to Hitler and Nazism. We can learn from their experience: may Christians today make their political-social decisions with a broader cultural awareness and greater sensitivity to the spirit of Christ.

Footnotes

1.   Paul Althaus, <u>Die Deutsche Stunde der
     Kirche</u>, 3rd ed. (Göttingen, 1934), p.
     5.

2.   <u>Ibid.</u>

3.   <u>Ibid.</u>, quoted by Althaus.

4.   See, for example, S. William Halperin,
     <u>Germany Tried Democracy: A Political
     History of the Reich from 1918-1933</u>
     (New York, 1946, 1965).

5.   The events leading up to World War I
     were complicated by nationalistic
     rivalries, colonialism, an arms race,
     and a system of treaty commitments which
     inexorably turned a small incident into
     a world war. To single out Germany as
     the villain was almost certainly unfair.

6.   For a description of Weimar Germany, see
     Walter Laqueur, <u>Weimar: A Cultural
     History 1918-1933</u> (New York, 1974), or
     Peter Gay, <u>Weimar Culture: The
     Outsider as Insider</u> (New York, 1968).

7.   See Hans-Walter Krumwiede, <u>Geschichte
     des Christentums III. Neuzeit: 17.
     bis 20. Jahrhundert</u> (Stuttgart,
     Kohlhammer, 1977), pp. 192-202.

8.   Krumwiede gives this figure to represnt
     that portion of the Protestant clergy
     which was anti-Weimar. It may not be
     exact -- finding the basis for exact
     calculation on these matters is difficult
     if not impossible -- but it accurately
     reflects both widespread dissatisfaction
     with Weimar and widespread acceptance of
     Hitler's rise.

9.   See Krumwiede, pp. 122-194.

10. William Nicholls, Systematic and
     Philosophical Theology (Harmondsworth,
     Middlesex, 1969), provides a useful
     introduction to modern theological
     issues. See also, Heinz Zahrnt, Die
     Sache mit Gott. Die protestantische
     Theologie im 20. Jahrhundert (Munich,
     1970).

11. This is point four of a ten-part
     program, quoted in Ernst Wolf, Barmen.
     Zwischen Versuchung und Gnade.
     Zweite, mit einem Nachwort und einem
     Personenregister, erweiterte Auflage
     (Munich, 1970).

12. Ibid.

13. Ibid.

14. Krumwiede explains the juxtaposition of
     the March 5 elections and Hitler's March
     23 speech, p. 214, in this fashion.

15. Quoted in Krumwiede, p. 214.

16. I am indebted to Krumwiede, pp. 211-241,
     for clarification of this sequence of
     events in 1933 and 1934. Klaus Scholder
     has written a major study of the church
     struggle up to June, 1934, Die Kirchen

und das Dritte Reich. Bd. 1: Vorgeschichte und Zeit der Illusionen 1918-1934 (Stuttgart, 1977). J.R.C. Wright's book, Above Parties: The Political Attitudes of the German Protestant Church Leadership 1918-1933 (Oxford, 1977), gives a good account of the climactic events in early 1933. John Conway provides a definitive study of the church struggle throughout the years of the Third Reich in his book, The Nazi Persecution of the Churches, 1933-1945 (London, 1968). See also, Ernst C. Helmreich, The German Churches under Hitler: Background, Struggle and Epilogue (Detroit, 1979).

17. See pp. 19-26.

18. This and subsequent quotation from documents of the Barmen Synod are taken from Arthur C. Cochrane, The Church' Confession under Hitler (Philadelphia: The Westminster Press, 1962), Appendix VII, pp. 237-247. See also Gerhard Niemöller, Die erste Bekenntnissynode der Deutschen Evangelischen Kirche zu Barmen, vol. II (Göttingen: Vandenhoeck & Ruprecht, 1959), pp. 196-206.

19. See Cochrane, note 5., p. 241.

20. Gerhard Niemöller, Die erste Bekenntnissynode der Deutschen Evangelischen Kirche zu Barmen, vol. I (Göttingen, Vandenhoeck & Ruprecht, 1959), p. 145. The entire "Ansbacher Ratschlag" is reprinted in this collection of documents.

21. Ibid., p. 171.

22. Ibid.

23. See Paul Althaus, "Gedanken zur
     'Theologischen Erlärung' der Barmer
     Erkenntnissynode," Korrespondenzblatt
     für die evangelischlutherischen
     Geistlichen in Bayern, #28 (July 9,
     1934), reprinted in Niemöller, Vol. I,
     pp. 168-170.

24. Ibid.

25. Krumwiede, p. 217.

26. The Marburg Gutachten was published in
     Theologische Blätter, vol. 12, #10
     (October 1933), pp. 289-294.

27. Hirsch's Gutachten on the Aryan
     paragraph was sent to the DEK leadership
     in Oct., 1933, and published in 1934:
     "Theologisches Gutachten in der
     Nichtarierfrage," Deutsche Theologie,
     #5 (May, 1934), pp. 182-199. Kittel
     made a broad statement against Jewish
     participation in virtually any public
     role in Germany in Die Judenfrage, 3rd
     ed. (Stuttgart, 1934). See also his
     correspondence with Karl Barth, Ein
     theologischer Briefwechsel (Stuttgart,
     1934).

28. See Paul Althaus and Werner Elert,
     "Theologische Gutachten über die
     Zulassung von Christen jüdischer
     Herkunft zu den Ämtern der deutschen
     evangelischen Kirche," Theologische
     Blätter, vol. 12, #11 (November,
     1933), pp. 321-324.

29. Dietrich Bonhöffer, "Die Kirche vor der
     Judenfrage," Gesammelte Schriften,
     vol. 2, pp. 44-53.

30.   Quoted in Krumwiede, p. 219.

31.   See Robert P. Ericksen, "Theologian in
      the Third <u>Reich</u>:   The Case of Gerhard
      Kittel," <u>Journal of Contemporary
      History</u>, vol. 12 (1977), pp. 595-622,
      or Ericksen, "Zur Auseinandersetzung mit
      und um Gerhard Kittels Antisemitismus,"
      <u>Evangelische Theologie</u>, vol. 43
      (1983), pp. 250-270.   The careers of
      Kittel, Althaus and Hirsch will all be
      considered in my forthcoming book at the
      Yale University Press, tentatively
      titled, <u>Theologians under Hitler:
      Gerhard Kittel, Paul Althaus and
      Emanuel Hirsch</u>.

THE GERMAN CHURCH STRUGGLE:
ITS MAKING AND MEANING

J.S. Conway

Fifty years after the Nazis took over power in Germany on 30 January 1933, the subsequent German Church Struggle is still of vital concern to historians, political scientists, and theologians. The flood of books, articles, sermons, pamphlets and other media treatment, which still continues, is evidence of this widespread interest.[1] Yet, despite these publications, the passage of time inevitably increases the difficulties of our understanding of these now far-off events, and also assists the growth of myths and misconceptions. The <u>Kirchenkampf</u> is still sometimes seen in terms of a classical conflict between Church and State, between Christianity and paganism, between democratic liberalism and Nazi intolerance, in short between good and evil. But, in fact, the history of these events, as in so many other cases, cannot so easily be depicted in black and white terms. Rather, we are now more fully aware of the many cross-currents, countervailing pressures and misperceived illusions, which present a very mottled picture of varying hues. How else can the frequent ambivalences about the role of the churches in this period of political turmoil be explained? Half a century later, it becomes all the more necessary to elucidate the long-range implications of the German Church Struggle and to seek to establish the significance of these events, not merely for the German churches alone, but for the wider ecumenical fellowship in the late twentieth century.

The initial paradox consists of the fact that no one at the beginning of 1933 wanted to become involved in a Church Struggle. The vast majority of German churchmen, both

Protestant and Catholic, welcomed Hitler's
accession to power. The crisis of identity
caused by the political changes imposed in
1918 had produced a sense of uncertainty as
to how the witness of the church could be
presented. The disillusionment of the
post-war generations had severely affected
the credibility of the Gospel message. The
impact of the Depression had further weakened
the capacity to restore Germany's economy or
national prestige. Increasingly, the rapid
success of the Nazi Party, with its appeal to
national revival, repudiation of the shame of
Versailles, rejection of Boshevism, and a new
moral tone in public life, found support from
churchmen throughout the country. Possibly
most influential of all was Hitler's
successful projection of himself as a strong
leader or father figure. The Catholic desire
to return to an authoritarianism of the
pre-Enlightenment period was matched by the
Protestant longings for a restoration of the
monarchy, or, if not, then of a substitute
figure. The wishful thinking for a leader
capable of uniting the whole people by his
decisiveness and popular appeal played an
important role in bringing to Hitler the
support of most churchmen. Indeed, by 1932,

some of the more enthusaistic clergymen in
the Protestant ranks were already calling for
a still more whole-hearted devotion to this
messianic figure. The Führer, they claimed
was

the redeemer in the history of the
Germans. Hitler stood there like a
rock in a wide desert, like an
island in an endless sea. In the
darkest night of our Christian
church history, Hitler became for
our time that marvellous
transparency, the window through
whom light fell on the history of
Christianity.[2]

The evidence is clear that, for the
first six months after the Nazi takeover of
power, such sentiments were widespread.[3]
Only a handful of pastors, most of them
already connected with extremely left-wing
political movements, resisted the allurements
of this modern Pied Piper of Hamelin.

It is equally notable that in 1933
Hitler and his principal advisors were also
reluctant   to embark on a conflict with the

churches. Hitler had earlier on realised the value of an indifferent or neutral pose towards religion. In 1920 the Nazi Party programme had advocated the vague promise of a "positive Christianity" without spelling out what that meant. Following his abortive coup in 1923, Hitler had deliberately recognised the need to placate such potential opponents as the churches. He saw that he could possibly win power without the churches, but not against them. Subsequently, he had dismissed the outspoken Gauleiter Dinter, who advocated an anti-clerical and anti-Christian paganism as the regenerative force for Nazi ideology. Hitler also gave no open support to the controversial and combative views of Alfred Rosenberg, the editor of his Party newspaper, the <u>Volkischer Beobachter</u>, on the subject of religion.

Following his take-over of power, Hitler's political requirement was to convince the majority of his countrymen that he was indeed the father-figure for whom they longed. His early speeches were notably conservative and reassuring in their assertion that the existing order of society would not be changed. The deliberate staging of the reopening of the Reichstag with an imposing church service on 23 March, 1933, in the Garrison Church in Potsdam, attended by the revered President Hindenburg, in which leading members of the Evangelical Church took part, was designed to strengthen this impression. It was followed within a week by the reopening of negotiations with the Catholic Church for the conclusion of a Reich Concordat, which Hitler saw would be a significant strengthening of his regime by gaining the international recognition of the Vatican. Such moves were, of course, tactically motivated. Hitler's aim was to seek the voluntary Gleichschaltung of all potential opponents and their subordination to the Nazis' unchallenged domination of the political scene. The Churches, he believed, would recognise their national duty, and he was duly gratified by the warm expressions of support given by such outstanding figures as Cardinals Bertram and Faulhaber in those early months.

It was all the more remarkable therefore that, in the latter half of 1933, there arose signs of tension within the churches which by

1934 were to harden into the conflict known as the Church Struggle. These initial stages were unanticipated and reluctantly entered into by both Protestants and Catholics, almost all of whom wanted to stress their continuing loyalty to the new regime. In the Evangelical Churches, the battle began over purely internal measures for ecclesiastical reorganisation. In June 1933 proposals were put forward for a new national church structure to coordinate the work of the twenty-eight provincial churches, under the leadership of a Reich Bishop. This plan was promoted by a group of younger radical clergymen, known as the Deutsche Christen, who were disillusioned by what they considered to be the elitist, old-guard set of leaders who had steered the church affairs since the defeat of 1918. In part, these men were opportunists believing that the new structure would open up positions of power, which they had previously been denied. In part, however, they claimed to be spear-heading a national revival and reinvigoration in the churches similar to that undertaken in the state by the Nazi Party. Their candidate for the Reich Bishopric was Ludwig Müller, a former army chaplain and reputed to enjoy Hitler's personal confidence. Under his leadership, the Deutsche Christen claimed, the church would march hand in hand with the State under the slogan: "the swastika on our breasts, and the Cross in our hearts."[4] Despite justified doubts in many quarters of Müller's competence, he was catapulted into the post at the end of June, and immediately called for national church elections. The Deutsche Christen seized the opportunity for a massive propaganda campaign and even enlisted Hitler's support to give a radio talk on their behalf. The result was a predictable and overwhelming victory.

The manner of Müller's appointment had raised objections, but the ground-swell grew louder when he announced his intention to follow the State's lead in introducing into the church's structures the so-called "Aryan paragraph" by which Germans of Jewish descent would be declared ineligible for office in the church, and those pastors already ordained would be required to resign. This assertion of Nazi racialist ideology over evangelical theology immediately aroused strong dissent. One of the leading pastors

of Berlin, Martin Niemöller, mobilised
supporters into the Pastors' Emergency League
in order to defend the traditional orthodox
Protestant doctrine against such innovative
heresies. In November, a further frontal
attack by the Deutsche Christen on such
elements of Christian teaching as the Old
Testament, and their demand for a thorough
purging of all Jewish practices and
vocabulary from the church's liturgies, won
enormous support to Niemöller's
counter-movement.

The Pastors' Emergency League was
forged and fostered by the sense of outrage
among a large proportion of the Evangelical
clergy - by the end of 1933 some 7,000, or
about one-third of the total had declared
their support. They were offended by the
raucous and radical attempts to politicise
their solemn assemblies by Nazi propaganda
methods. Niemöller's efforts to mobilise
pressure to secure the removal of the new
Reich Bishop Müller and the reversal of his
policies of forcible Gleichschaltung,
however, proved unavailing. Attempts were
then made at the highest political level by
interventions with President Hindenburg,

which led to an audience between twelve of
the prominent leaders of the Evangelical
Churches and Hitler personally on 25 January,
1934. Contrary to their hope, however, that
Hitler could be persuaded to disavow Müller
and his measures, the Führer turned the
tables by a violent attack on Niemöller as a
"turbulent priest," and charged the bishops
with disloyalty to the state. Under the
impact of these accusations, a declaration of
solidarity with Müller was demanded and
obtained. Or, as Hitler himself later
recalled,

> The representatives of the
> Evangelical Church were so shaken
> that they literally collapsed, to
> the point of becoming dumb and
> invisible.[5]

Taking advantage of this situation, the
Deutsche Christen under Müller's
leadership attempted to coerce the various
provincial churches into strict obedience to
his authoritarian fiats. In September and
October 1934, the Evangelical Bishops of
Würtemberg and Bavaria were suspended from
office, placed under house arrest and their

duties forcibly taken over with the aid of
the police. Not surprisingly, these moves
caused a storm of protest by their loyal
parishioners. Huge meetings were held in
churches throughout the provinces, and in the
end Hitler was forced to intervene personally
to order the release of the bishops and their
reinstatement in office. "Mountains of
telegrams, representations from the
deaneries, and entreaties of evey sort" had
been sent to Berlin and forced the Nazis to
recognise the wholly unfortunate consequences
of this confrontation. In fact, this episode
showed how popular opinion, in this case
steered and orchestrated by the Protestant
clergy, could inflict a major political
defeat even in the restrictive conditions of
a repressive police state.[6]

On the other hand, this episode also
shows the limits of such public protest. The
defence of two highly popular bishops in the
name of traditional orthodoxy had united all
those who resented interference from Berlin,
or any attack on their favoured practices.
It did not mean any lessening of the basic
loyalty felt towards Hitler personally or the
nationalistic policies he was pursuing.

Indeed, Hitler's intervention and rectification of the situation enhanced his personal prestige, while the disillusionment was focussed on to his underlings.

The same dichotomy of views could be observed among the members of the Pastors' Emergency League. While vigorously opposing the authoritarian attempts to suppress their opposition to Müller's arbitrary interventions, Niemöller and his followers still professed complete loyalty to the Nazi State, as for example in October 1933 when Neimöller sent Hitler a telegram of congratulations on his decision to withdraw Germany from the League of Nations. The realisation that Nazi totalitarian goals were more far-reaching in their implications was only very slowly and reluctantly accepted by the church authorities, who continued to believe that Nazism and Christianity could be combined in a harmonious blend of loyalties.

There were, however, those who realised that any effective opposition to the Nazi dictatorship in church affairs would have to be more soundly based. For this reason, Bishop Wurm of Württemberg summoned a

conference in April 1934 to lay the
foundations of an alternative church
structure, which came to be known as the
Confessing Church, under the leadership of a
Reich Council of Brethren. These men saw
that the prime requisite for the
establishment of a rival authority was a
theological statement which would clearly
define the church's integrity and its right
to control its own affairs. The result was
the famous Barmen Declaration of May 1934,
largely inspired by the ideas of Professor
Karl Barth of Bonn University. Barth had
earlier established his reputation as the
orginator of the so-called "dialectic
theology," which strongly attacked the
Kulturprotestantismus of the preceding
years, whereby theology had too often served
as a form of spirtual justification of
contemporary political ideas. In Barth's
view, the Deutsche Christen had now
carried this tendency forward to the point
where they were seeking to validate the
heretical and anti-Christian ideology of
National Socialism. The "true" church must
take its stand on the orthodox traditions of
Reformation theology and reject, in particular,

all totalitarian claims of the State both on
the Church and in the political field.

This determination to prevent the church
from becoming the propaganda weapon of any
political movement was matched by an equal
desire to alert the church against an
uncritical acceptance of submission to the
ruling powers, based on a one-sided
interpretation of Romans 13. The inclination
of many of the more pietist circles in
Lutheranism to confine their commitment to a
purely "spiritual" realm and to deny any need
for political or social engagement was here
forcefully challenged. On the other hand,
the Barmen Confession was not intended to be
a political protest against the Nazi State.
The Confessing Church never became a
spearhead of resistance to the tyranny which
engulfed Germany, and the ambivalences were
never resolved between those who still
believed that Church and State could
cooperate in a united stand, and those who
saw more clearly the fatefulness of the Nazi
ambitions.

By 1935 it was clear that the Nazi goal
of subordinating all the Evangelical Churches

to the Party line was not succeeding. Not
only had the staunch minority of the
Confessing Church laid the basis for an
alternative structure of church government,
but it had armed itself with a coherent
theological position which could be used to
rebut the heretical excesses of the
Deutsche Christen. The incompetence and
ineptitude of the Reich Bishop and his
followers not only provoked strong opposition
but revealed to the world the lack of unity
in this important section of the community.
Unwelcome attention was being drawn in the
foreign press and among foreign diplomats to
the quarrels caused by this Church Struggle,
as, for example, could be seen in the
interventions sent to the German Foreign
ministry after the arrest of the South German
bishops. This totally contradicted the image
of a united nation which the Nazis sought to
project abroad. Even more serious was the
consideration that such groups might become
the focus point of a new opposition to the
Nazi ambitions throughout society. It was
time for a new beginning.

In July 1935 Hitler ordered the
establishment of a new Ministry of Religious

Affairs.   This unprecedented step was
designed to mobilise the State's power to
enforce Gleichschaltung on the warring
factions.   In effect it meant the suppression
and discrediting of Reich Bishop Müller, who
thereafter disappeared into the shadows.   But
the net result was, in effect, no better.
Unable to coerce by force so large and
popular a section of the community, the Reich
Ministry sought to use a carrot and stick
policy to compel obedience and to force the
disputatious clergymen to toe the line.   The
new Minister, Hanns Kerrl, an old crony of
Hitler's, believed that theological
hair-splitting could be left to the pastors,
so long as all recognised that true
Christianity and National Socialism were
identical:

> Adolph Hitler has hammered into the
> hearts of the German People both
> the faith and the fact of Jesus.
> The people are now awake and want
> to be led by us and by no one
> else.[7]

The Churches had no business interfering in
politics, which did not belong in the

pulpits. His Ministry would seek to control
all the external factors of the churches'
life and thus avoid the unseemly disunity of
earlier years.

But Kerrl soon found that his so-called
mediating task was sabotaged on all sides.
The Confessing Church leaders had serious and
continuing reservations about the misuse of
the state's power over doctrinal issues and
refused to accept that Kerrl could decide
what constituted true Christian loyalty. But
also, on the other side, many of the more
radical Nazi leaders were sceptical of any
such attempt to bring the church into line
with Nazi ideology and instead sought to root
out the churches' influence altogether.
Kerrl proved incapable of controlling the
nefarious activities of more powerful rivals
in the Party, such as Bormann or Heydrich,
and was constantly frustrated by the fact
that even his good intentions were cancelled
out by the more extreme anti-clerical
measures of the Gestapo and other Nazi
agencies. In 1941, he died, a disillusioned
and defeated man. He was not replaced.

These rivalries and internecine feuds within the Nazi Party over the implementation of the Church Struggle were only partially realized by its victims. There was just enough uncertainty about the Nazi intentions, reinfored by plenty of wishful thinking, to make many of the Confessing Church leaders believe that a policy of accommodation and avoidance of all political activities could lead to their survival intact. But from 1935 onwards, this view was challenged by those in the Confessing Church who rightly saw that such an accommodation could only be achieved by a betrayal of the Gospel. The attempt to draw a rigid line between church and secular affairs and loyalties was no longer relevant in face of a totalitarian force such as the Nazis presented. The followers of Martin Niemöller were constantly dismayed by the readiness to compromise of other sections of the Confessing Church, such as those led by Bishop Marahrens of Hannover, let alone by the enthusiastic panegyrics of the Deutsche Christen. Neimöller's arrest and incarceration in 1937 only confirmed this split, while depriving the Confessing Church of its most combative figure. All sections of the Evangelical Churches, however, continued to stress their staunch support for Hitler's nationalist goals. Inevitably, their protests became more muted with the approach of war, and they readily welcomed the signs after 1939 that the Church Struggle was to be put on ice for the duration of the war, so that all could unite behind the war effort. To the end, even strong believers in the theological position of the Confessing Church continued to think that Hitler was not responsible for the excesses of anti-clericalism, anti-church administrative restrictions, or anti-Christian outbursts from Nazi propagandists. These were ascribed to radical hotheads lower down in the party ranks, which would be corrected if only the Führer knew about them. It was hardly surprising that only a tiny handful of Evangelical churchmen, most prominently Dietrich Bonhoeffer, joined the ranks of the German Resistance, or understood the true dimensions of the revolutionary character of the Third Reich.

II

Among German Catholics, the same pattern can be observed of enthusiastic endorsation

of the new regime in the early months of
1933, followed by uncertainty and dismay in
the later months. There is no reason to
doubt the sincerity of the Catholic bishops'
praise of Hitler for so rapidly concluding
the Reich Concordat in 1933, which they all
believed would not only secure Catholic
rights previously in doubt, but even add new
ones. Cardinal Faulhaber wrote to Hitler on
24 July 1933 as follows:

> Your statesmanlike far-sightedness
> had achieved in six months what the
> old parliaments and parties failed
> to achieve in sixty years... This
> agreement with the Head of the
> Church can bring for the inner life
> of the German people, through the
> securing of religious freedom, an
> increase of faith and with it an
> increase of the ethical power of
> the people.[8]

The early reservations which the bishops
had felt lest, by remaining aloof from the
popular tide, they might be overrun by forces
they could not control, now seemed to be met
by the legalised provisions of the new

Concordat. Hitler himself, as he later
acknowledged,[9] had seen the risk that the
Concordat and the expectations it aroused
might prove to be a hindrance to his
subsequent course of action. Indeed, had the
churches been able to insist that these
promises were kept, the whole Nazi claim to
total power would have been challenged if not
prevented. But, with his intuitive
understanding of the political forces at work
among his opponents, Hitler calculated, quite
rightly, that he would be able to outflank the
Church's leaders and, in his own time, would
be able to revoke, or evade, the concessions
which now appeared to be offered so
generously.

By the end of the summer of 1933, Hitler
recognised that the balance of forces was
much more in his favour. The open support
given by the Catholic bishops and by the Pope
to his regime would now make it very
difficult for them to reverse their stand and
admit that they had been mistaken. The
likelihood of an outright condemnation by the
Church, similar to those seen in Mexico or
the Soviet Union, was now ruled out.
Nevertheless, he had no intention of allowing

himself to be entrapped or hampered in his goal of securing total control over all aspects of German public life. On the one hand, Hitler recognised the danger of repeating Bismarck's attempted suppression of the Catholics in the <u>Kulturkampf</u> of the 1870s. On the other hand, any permanent accommodation between Nazi ideology and Catholicism, along the lines Mussolini had taken in Italy, was unthinkable, if only because, among large numbers of the Nazi supporters, anti-clericalism was almost as rampant as anti-semitism.

Hitler therefore adopted the shrewd strategy of professing his opposition solely to "political Catholicism". By appealing to the nationalism of Catholics over the heads of their bishops, the Nazis asserted that the measures taken to control or limit the church's influence in German life were only directed to curbing anti-German habits of mind, or "jesuitical" influences imported from Rome. While the Nazis were unable to count on the support of any significant number of priests, in contrast to the uncritical adulation of the Protestant <u>Deutsche Christen</u>, they also knew that

the bishops would hesitate before forcing
their followers to choose between loyalty to
the Church, or allegiance to the new German
state and Party.

The Catholic Church Struggle was
therefore conducted tactically as a war of
attrition. Hitler never repudiated the
Concordat, nor even renounced his own
personal standing as a (non-practising)
Catholic. Relations with the Vatican were
maintained throughout the Nazi era, and the
Papal Nuncio, though increasingly ineffective
and isolated, was never sent packing. On the
other hand, no steps were taken to impede the
lower level of Nazi officialdom from measures
designed to undermine the Catholic hold among
the people, either through inflammatory
speeches against specific Catholic doctrines,
or administrative measures designed to
curtail the church's public activities.

For their part, neither the Pope nor
the German bishops ever risked a total
confrontation or condemnation of the Nazi
government. As Gordon Zahn has noted, German
Catholics were never taught at any time
during the Nazi era to recognise the demonic

nature of the Nazi regime.[10]   Instead the
German Catholic bishops only reluctantly gave
up their illusions about the promise of
whole-hearted collaboration, and some, even
to the end, such as the Presiding Bishop,
Cardinal Bertram, continued to express his
loyalty to the appointed Head of State.

Likewise, the Vatican prevaricated.
Although early on alerted to the Nazis'
totalitarian intentions, and fully aware of
the chicanery with which they were
circumventing or negating the provisions of
the Concordat, the Vatican officials
continued to hope that these were temporary
aberrations. The Pope and his advisers
continued to believe that the German dictator
could be brought to see reason in his church
policy. From the point of view of the
Vatican, Germany was too important a nation,
and the German Catholics too central in their
world-wide calculations, to be ejected from
the Catholic family because of the misdeeds
of a few hotheads. Consequently, the
Cardinal Secretary of State, Pacelli, who was
primarily responsible for the signing of the
Concordat in 1933, and who in 1939 was
elected Pope as Pius XII, continued to

protest privately against the infringements
of the Concordat by the German government or
the ideological "errors" of Nazi propaganda
attacks on the Church, but at the same time
to hope for a negotiated settlement with
Hitler and his minions. It was, as Klaus
Scholder has rightly remarked, a policy based
on a false judgement. But it was shared by
other powers besides the Holy See. Indeed
all Europe made the same miscalculation.[11]

The Catholic Church Struggle was
therefore conducted by the Nazis as a form of
cat and mouse chase. No open conflict with
the church on the lines of the Kulturkampf
was declared. No sweeping measures against
all the bishops or congregations were
edicted. No interference with church
services was attempted. But the Gestapo had
free rein to arrest or discipline any
Catholic priest or lay leader whose loyalty
to the new regime seemed to be a threat to
the party's position. And no barriers were
placed against rabid ideological speeches by
Nazi Party agitators, which sought to
penetrate and counteract the Catholic way of
life. From 1933 onward, the Nazis' main
target was the young people. The Nazi Youth

Leader, Baldur von Schirach, for example, led
a massive campaign to win over the members of
Catholic youth organisations to his own
Hitler Youth.   In November 1934 he
proclaimed: "The way of Rosenberg is the way
for German youth," and denounced the Catholic
youth organisations as separatist and
disloyal.[12]   In 1935, in the Rhineland, a
"spring offensive" was declared, which by
using both propaganda and terroristic
tactics, was designed to force the Catholic
organisations to dissolve altogether.
Pressure was put on parents to do their
"duty" by enrolling their children in the
Hitler Youth.   Following the prohibition of
dual membership, this automatically would
exclude these children from rival Catholic
groups.

At the same time, orders were given to
disband other Catholic lay organisations
which traditionally had catered for church
social life. Pilgrimages, retreats or other
social festivities which had been part and
parcel of the rural society for centuries
were either prohibited or restricted on the
flimsiest of excuses. The priests were
commanded to confine their activities solely

to those which took place inside the church
buildings. And there were innumerable cases
where direct intimidation by Nazi thugs
sought to frighten both priests and people
into submission. If, at first, these
instances were believed by the bishops to be
no more than isolated cases of anti-clerical
bigotry by the revolutionary fervour of
individual Nazis, the volume of complaints
which came in to all the church leaders soon
made it clear that here was a national
campaign, orchestrated and encouraged on the
highest level.

Despite their advantages of having both
the power of the police and the propaganda
machinery of the State at their command, the
Nazis were soon to find that the resistance
of the Catholics was unyielding. Eager and
willing as the majority of Catholics
undoubtedly were to support the government in
its foreign policy, its repudiation of
democracy, its persecution of Communists and
Jews, and its revitalisation of the nation's
economy, they refused to accept the
all-demanding claims of the Party in matters
so closely affecting their religious life.
Despite all the propaganda, Catholic youth

organisations continued to grow. Resolute
scepticism was shown about the Nazi claims to
be providing the moral guidance for the whole
community, especially in those areas where
the priest enjoyed a much fuller confidence
in the village than his Nazi counterpart,
often the local schoolteacher or innkeeper,
whose morals frequently left much to be
desired.

The determination of the Catholic milieu
to maintain its traditional place in the
community can be seen most clearly in the
resolute opposition to the Nazis'
iconoclastic attempts to enforce their ideas
of "secularisation" by the removal of the
outward signs of Catholic piety, such as
crucifixes or images, in public places. By
far the strongest resentment among Catholics
was aroused in the north German district of
Oldenburg in 1936, and again in Bavaria in
1941, when the Nazi leaders ordered the
removal of crucifixes from the schools. The
crucifix became the symbol of the struggle to
replace the Cross with the Swastika. But the
outraged protests of hundreds of Catholic
parents, especially mothers, in defence of
the Catholic schools, forced the Nazis to

retreat - a fact that was quickly known throughout the country.

This readiness to defend their historical institutions, values and traditions among churchmen constituted the most effective barrier to the Nazi aims of moulding the population into willing agents of its ideological goals. It was exactly these feelings that were to be aroused again in the still more famous protests of 1941 against the Nazi euthanasia campaign. Churchmen, both Catholic and Protestant, rallied to the leadership given by Bishop Count Galen of Münster. Their success in bringing to a virtual halt this ruthless murder of innocent men, women and children was largely due to its being regarded as an attack on the innate values of what Germans still considered to be a Christian society, and because it was their unfortunate relatives who were being "disposed of" for political reasons.

For their part, the Nazis drew the conclusion that the stubborn scepticism of the church congregations was largely due to the "obscurantism" of poisoning the

atmosphere against Nazism by their tireless
sniping in sermons or their constant visits
to individuals in their homes. In 1935 and
1936, therefore, a massive campaign was
launched to try and separate the priests from
the people. Gigantic propaganda exercises
were undertaken, accompanied by lurid
headlines in the Nazi newspapers, accusing the
clergy, especially monks and nuns, of sexual
crimes against children in their care, or
against church leaders for infringing the
currency laws by smuggling gold across
Germany's frontiers. No effort was spared to
denigrate these "criminals" and a number of
show trials were staged. The results were,
however, totally depressing for the Nazis. As
one disillusioned Nazi supporter wrote
anonymously to the Party headquarters after
some nuns were arbitrarily dismissed from the
local school in 1936:

> Which Catholic mother did not weep
> in the last few days when she was
> told about it by her children? I
> happened to be a witness as to how
> the children cried in the streets
> for their sisters, and all the
> grown-ups who came with them. Must

the sisters go to make way again
for Nazi bosses, or because they
are Catholic? In fifty years time
the children will still have fond
memories of their good sisters,
while certainly no one will give a
damn about these Nazi bosses
whether they disappear today or
tomorrow...

P.S. Would the wicked Communists
have attacked us in such a way?[13]

In the face of such attacks, the solidarity
of the clergy and people was not undermined,
but rather reinforced. The police reports on
such incidents were almost universally
negative, concluding that the net result was
a still greater alienation of the population
from Nazi goals, at least in this particular
sphere.

This vigorous defence of the church's
interests had, however, its limitations.
Where the Church struggle could be seen as an
attack on local and visible targets, much
treasured and beloved by the local
populations, some success, or at least a
postponement of defeat, might be achieved.

But on the wider sphere, and at a national level, the results were more uncertain. The Catholic hierarchy of bishops, like the majority of the Evangelical church, both leaders, including those of the Confessing Church, continued to stress their loyalty to the regime. As the Bavarian bishops declared in December 1936:

> Nothing could be further from our intentions than to adopt a hostile attitude towards, or a renunciation of, the present form taken by our government. For us, respect for authority, love of Fatherland, and the fulfilment of our duty to the State are matters not only of conscience, but of divine ordinance... The Führer can be certain that we bishops are prepared to give all moral support to his historic struggle against Bolshevism. We will not criticise things which are purely political. What we do ask is that our Holy Church be permitted to enjoy her God-given rights and her freedom.[14]

The consequent ambivalence about where the line should be drawn between the things that were God's and the things that were Caesar's placed a continuing barrier on any really effective growth of opposition in church ranks. The more farsighted clergy and laymen felt constantly frustrated by the passivity of the bishops and by the attempt to retain a legalistic approach to the safeguards of the Concordat. In the eyes of a more militant minority, a much less accommodating policy would be necessary to counteract the unscrupulous chicanery of the Nazis, who had clearly shown their contempt for the law and their readiness to conduct the Church Struggle by all means, fair or foul. On the other hand, the bishops could not fail to note that the majority of their followers had no wish, or training, for any large-scale campaign of civil disobedience. There was no tradition of mobilising congregations in defence of such issues as human rights, especially of non-churchmen, such as the Jews. And those church leaders, such as Bishops Galen of Münster and von Preysing of Berlin, who most strongly opposed the Nazis as unprincipled upstarts, were

themselves the most conservative believers in
an authoritarian nationalism and fully
accepted the Nazi view of Germany's
threatened position in the world.

The Catholic Church Struggle was at best
a reluctant and half-hearted affair. Only in
the ideological sphere could there be no
quarter given. Churchmen and Nazis agreed
that Christianity and National Socialism were,
in the long run, incompatible. But both sides
were to be disillusioned in their attempts to
gain the total commitment of the population
to this point of view. On the Catholic side,
the most notable failure can be seen with the
publication of the Papal Encyclical <u>Mit
Brennender Sorge</u> of March 1937. This move
had been the result of the desire of the
German bishops to call to their aid the
supreme voice of the church, and to bolster
their position through the words of the Pope
himself. By highly skilful and secret
organisation, this Encyclical was distributed
and read in all Catholic parishes throughout
Germany without the Gestapo being able to
intervene. It denounced in no uncertain
terms the neo-paganism of Nazi racial ideas,
reaffirmed Catholic teachings, and called for

loyalty to the traditional doctrines of the Church. But the results were disappointing. For the Encyclical failed to stop the Nazi campaign of harassment and intimidation. More serious was the luke-warm response of the Catholic population, who still continued to believe that they could be both good Catholics and good Nazis in all other areas of political involvement. In matters directly affecting Catholic interests, the population could be aroused to defend its traditional rights and privileges; but on such questions of national expansion, hatred of unwanted minorities, or infringement of personal liberties, the Catholic reponse was at best muted and aloof.

On the other hand, the Nazis' lack of success was equally notable. The Nazis failed to break the allegiance of churchmen to their specific religious ties. Despite all the efforts at propagandistic indoctrination, particularly of the young, the Nazi ideology never made any significant headway. To the dismay of the chief proponents of Nazism, such as Rosenberg, Himmler, or Bormann 95% of the population still maintained their allegiance to the

Christian churches. After the outbreak of war, political tactics demanded the rallying of all sections of the population to the war effort, and, as a result, the ideological campaign had to be curtailed. The Church Struggle was therefore postponed until the German victory was assured. In the middle of the war, the Gestapo's church specialists were instructed to hold the line on further measures to counteract the churches' hold over the people. But at the same time they should ensure that the church leaders should not be allowed to claim an advantage from their "loyal" support of the war effort in order to gain more ground after the war was over. There can be little doubt that if the Nazis had been victorious, a much more vigorous Church Struggle would have ensued.

III

With the advantage of hindsight, we can see that the chief hindrance to any wider extension of the Church Struggle among the church-going population was their reluctance to realise the implications of the Nazi totalitarian challenge. Even those leaders who did realise the basic incompatibility of

Nazism and Christianity shared at least a partial identity of views of those of the abhorrent regime and supported many of its policies. Many churchmen were scandalised at the violent Nazi excesses, visible to all, such as the Crystal Night pogrom against the Jews of November 1938. But, in the main, this sense of outrage was more against the means than the ends. The notable failure to counteract the Nazi attacks upon the alleged pernicious influences of the Jews was largely due to the latent antisemitic ideas long present, in one form or another, in German minds, which the churches made virtually no effort to rectify. Consequently when the Nazis deported the Jews from sight, and no accurate knowledge could be gleaned about their fate, i.e. when secrecy covered the means by which this problem received its "final solution," no effective protest or opposition was forthcoming.

Similarly, the brutal treatment of other unwanted minorities, including the smaller religious sects, or the even more terrible atrocities inflicted on the peoples conquered during the war, aroused dismay or even concern among many well-meaning churchmen.

But they had no real objection to the ends
for which the Nazis claimed to be fighting,
and, still less, had any real alternative
pattern of political obligation to propose.
The whole weakness of the so-called German
resistance lay in the fact that it seldom
envisaged a different form of government, but
only the rectification of certain "mistakes"
of the Nazi leaders. This was certainly true
of all segments of the German educated elite,
including the churches. Driven from the
beginning into a position of defensiveness,
they never recovered the initiative or
fashioned the structures which alone could
have mobilised the churches into a valid
counterattack against Nazi totalitarianism.

During the Third Reich, the vast
majority of churchmen, like most of their
bourgeois counterparts, refused to believe
that they were embroiled in a revolutionary
process. Their wishful thinking led them to
ignore or excuse the Nazi excesses until it
was too late. Their nationalism and
adherence to doctrines of authority prevented
any large-scale organisation or protests
against the injustices of which they were
aware, and discouraged critical attention to

others being perpetrated in the name of Germany in the closed world of the occupied territories during the war. Rather, churchmen readily enough accepted at face value the Nazis' public statements, and failed to see that the Church Struggle and even more blatant persecution of the Jews were part and parcel of a drive to radicalise all previous traditional social structures through the imposition of racialist creed by political means. One by one the Nazis intended to eliminate their opponents, either by ruthless force, trickery, or induced capitulation. This tragic miscalculation of the German churches was later ruefully recalled by Martin Niemöller:

> When they arrested the Communists and Socialists, I said: I am not a Communist, so I did nothing. When they imprisoned the Jews, I said: I am not a Jew, so I did nothing. When they attacked the Catholics, I said: I am not a Catholic, so I did nothing. When they came for me, there was no one left.[15]

The majority of German churchmen never realised that the Nazi social revolution was meant to be more than a mere restoration of authoritarian patterns of leadership. It was in fact far more radical, and was to be achieved in four stages: first by the Gleichschaltung of political institutions, then by control over social organisations, thirdly by the manipulation of individual and family structures, and finally by the radical alteration of the concept of law. The first stage took place in 1933-1934 with the forcible amalgamation of the provincial governments, the abolition of the political parties, the emasculation of the Reichstag and the disappearance of the Reich Presidency. The second, more far-reaching and disruptive stage led to the efforts made to abolish social differences by propaganda attacks on all "reactionary" or traditional social institutions such as the churches, to be replaced by a united loyalty to Hitler under the slogan: Ein Reich, Ein Volk, Ein Führer. The successful appeal to national loyalties, to xenophobia and to racial bigotry undoubtedly encouraged in many minds the alienation from inherited attachments and standards. The sad tale of capitulation and compromise which marked the response of the civil service, the universities, the school system, the press, the judicature, the trade unions and even the churches produced few insurmountable barriers. Even though, as we have noted, this process was not entirely successful, the propaganda victories produced by a captive press, harnessed to a single-minded state ideology, cannot be regarded as insignificant. By constantly playing upon the disarray in the Protestant ranks, and by exploiting the latent anticlericalism of many nominal Catholics, the Nazis succeeded in preventing any united or coherent opposition.

These attacks upon the autonomy of public and visible institutions of German society were matched by the equally ambitious and determined campaign to control the private lives of individuals. The manipulation of Germany's young people was particularly designed to break down family loyalties and implant the germinal cells of the fully totalitarian state of the future. Political indoctrination and social pressures were consistently combined to preclude German youths and their parents from any association

with dangerous influences, such as Jews or
the Churches' youth organisations.

The fourth stage of this social
revolution was to be attained in the radical
alteration of the concept of law. In
essence, the Nazis sought to sweep away all
previous practices and safeguards for the
individual and substitute the dynamic ideas
of the Führer's will. Hitler was to become
the supreme judge of the nation - as already
claimed on the occasion of the murders of
Röhm and his supporters in June 1934. The
later President of the People's Court,
another Nazi invention, Roland Freisler, made
this doctrine his <u>leitmotiv</u>, as could be
seen in the scandalous so-called "trials" of
the organisers of the 20 July 1944 plot
against Hitler's life. In sentencing to
death one of the participants, Count Helmuth
von Moltke, Freisler clearly stated the Nazi
totalitarian aim:

> Count Moltke, Christianity and
> National Socialism have one thing
> in common and one thing only: we
> claim the whole man.[16]

In the Nazi occupied territories of Poland and the Soviet Union, the existing structures and legal systems were systematically abolished. Simultaneously the Nazi racial policies were implemented. The institutionalisation of the Nazi racial theories found their fulfilment in the concentration camps and extermination programmes in Auschwitz, Treblinka and Maidanek. There can be little doubt that they were intended to be the pattern for later introduction to the whole of the Third Reich.

Only a few churchmen saw, at the time, where this process of concentrating power into the hands of an all-controlling bureaucracy could lead. The churches, like other segments of Germany's traditional society, were led by men who sought to limit the ferocity of the attacks made on them by policies of accommodation designed to prevent "worse excesses." Thrown on the defensive by the speed and success of the Nazi Gleichschaltung, the defenders of the old order, in self-defence, came to limit their efforts to the maintenance of their own autonomy and to delude themselves into thinking that these fortresses of tradition could survive the onslaught of the modern state with all its resources for total control. Even where this attempt was organisationally successful, as with the Confessing Church, it was achieved by limiting the area to be defended, and so leaving in the lurch the Nazis' more defenceless victims, such as the Jews. Only Dietrich Bonhoeffer saw with clarity the close relationship between the attacks on the churches and the persecution of the Jews. To the astonishment of his students, on the occasion of the infamous Crystal Night in November 1938, Bonhoeffer perceptively pointed out: "If the synagogues burn today, the churches will be on fire tomorrow."[17]

To the Nazis, the inculcation of virulent anti-semitism and anti-clericalism, the incitement to fanaticism and cruelty, and the successful manipulation of the population by propaganda methods were the means of mobilising the energies and dynamic aggression of the German people in the service of the Führer's will. It was a dangerous illusion of the churches to believe that their numbers provided security or that

they could retreat into the sacristy and
isolate themselves from political
involvement. It was an even more dangerous
illusion to believe that the church could
escape from this process of Nazi social
revolution. By their support of Nazi war
aims, the churches became implicated with the
imperialist aggression against which they
roused no protest. Further, by failing to
erect barriers against anti-semitism in their
own congregations, the churches became
accessories to the unprecedented Nazi
atrocities against the Jews. By shutting
their eyes to the true nature of the Nazi
regime, the churches, like the majority of
other established institutions, contributed
to their own downfall. Only a few brave
voices were raised in protest against the
delusions of the majority, or against the
perversions and corruption of the Nazi state.
These few men and women, by warning their
fellow churchmen against active
participation or, at best, passive
acquiescence in these Nazi crimes, saved the
churches from total apostasy and
capitulation. It was the same men - or at
least those who survived - who so rightly
described their own shortcomings in the

famous Stuttgart Declaration of guilt of
October 1945:

> We have fought for long years in
> the name of Jesus Christ against
> the spirit that found horrible
> expression in the National
> Socialist regime of force; but we
> charge ourselves for not having
> borne testimony with greater
> courage, prayed more consciously,
> believed more joyously, and loved
> more ardently.[18]

The role of the churches in the German
Church Struggle too often displayed their
characteristic of personal frailty and
weakness. But equally significant were the
institutional failures. In the forty years
which have elapsed since the Church Struggle
ended, we have had time to reflect on its
meaning in both of these aspects.

Let me here conclude with two important
points.

First, the German Church struggle should
not be seen as merely a historical event

which can be safely relegated to the history textbooks. The issues then raised still have relevance today. Nothing in the subsequent generation can lead us to believe that the abuse or misuse of state power against which some of the Confessing Church protested has today become less of a danger to human life or to the faith of the church.

Second, the German Church Struggle was not just a German event. If it had been solely concerned to seek to maintain the German churches' position of privileges, the overthrow of the Nazi state might have sufficed. But, at the time, alert Church leaders, especially in the ecumenical movement, were aware of its wider significance. Since 1945, the realisation has grown stronger than the on-going collapse of every credible religious or moral restraint on the state, the extraordinarily powerful force of propaganda, the growth of dehumanising ideologies of various kinds, and the erosion of religious traditions, which were so evident during the Nazi era, and against which a part, at least, of the German churches protested, were and are social developments which are by no means confined to Germany. Perhaps the principal lesson of the German Church Struggle is to force a more clear-sighted realisation of how necessary it has now become to erect barriers against these pervasive and destructive forces of our modern times.

Footnotes

1. For the English-speaking reader, the
    most comprehensive accounts are: E.
    Helmreich, The German Churches under
    Hitler, Detroit 1979; G. Lewy, The
    Catholic Church and Nazi Germany, New
    York 1964; J.S. Conway, The Nazi
    Persecution of the Churches 1933-1945,
    London 1968.

2. see Hans Buchheim, Glaubenskrise im
    Dritten Reich: drei Kapitel
    nationalsozialistischen
    Religionspolitik, Stuttgart, 1953, p.
    51.

3. For example, a pastor in Cobourg
    recorded in his memoirs a typical
    reaction to one of Hitler's speeches:
    "Our hearts were deeply moved. It is as
    if the wing of a great turn of fate is
    fluttering above us. It was to be a new
    start": Pastor R. Rössler, quoted in
    I. Kershaw, Popular Opinion and
    Political Dissent in the Third Reich,
    Oxford 1983, p. 158.

4.   Conway, op. cit., p. 45.

5.   Hitler's Table Talk, ed. A. Bullock,
     London 1953, p. 413.

6.   Kershaw, op. cit., p. 174.

7.   Speech by Reich Minister Kerrl, 13
     February 1937, printed in K.D. Schmidt,
     Dokumente des Kirchenkampfes, Vol. II,
     Goettingen 1965, pp. 1347-55.

8.   H. Müller, Katholische Kirche und
     Nationalsozialismus, Munich 1963, p.
     55.

9.   Hitler's Table Talk, entry for 13
     December 1941.

10. G. Zahn, German Catholics and Hitler's
     Wars, London 1963, p. 108.

11. K. Scholder, Die Kirchen und das Dritte
     Reich, Vol. I, Berlin 1977, p. 662.

12. see Conway, op. cit., p. 123.

13. quoted in Kershaw, op. cit., p. 211.

14. Documents on Nazism 1919-1945, ed. J.
     Noakes and G. Pridham, London 1974, p.
     372.

15. quoted frequently in Niemöller's
     speeches in the United States 1947.

16.   quoted in <u>Dying We Live</u>, ed., H. Gollwitzer, E. Kuhn and R. Schneider, London 1965, p. 121.

17.   Gottfried Maltusch, "When the Synogogues Burnt" in <u>I Knew Dietrich Bonhoeffer</u>, ed. W.D. Zimmerman and R.G. Smith, London 1966, p. 150. It was notable that these students, the cream of the Confessing Church's young people, could seriously consider this Nazi pogrom as the fulfilment of the curse which had haunted the Jews since Jesus' death on the cross. For a fuller treatment, see R. Gutteridge, <u>Open Thy Mouth for the Dumb. The German Evangelical Church and the Jews 1879-1950</u>. Oxford, 1976.

18.   S. Herman, <u>The Rebirth of the German Church</u>, London 1946, p. 137.

BARMEN: WHAT WE HAVE LEARNED AND WHAT WE HAVE YET TO LEARN

– Joseph Bettis

It is easier to tell what we have learned from Barmen than what we have yet to learn. We have already learned to loathe facism and other forms of modern totalitarianism. We have learned to value and respect the struggle of Jews to worship and live according to their traditions. We have learned to respect the people who struggled against the Third Reich in Germany and in other countries. We also have learned of the ease with which well-meaning people, even in the most cultivated circumstances,

can abet the actions of unscrupulous
political opportunists.

On the other hand, the changes in our
world in the fifty years since 1933 have been
so profound that the relevance of those past
events may be difficult to see. World War
II, the Holocaust, and the Church Struggle
marked the close of the era of the
nation-state and the collapse of the colonial
hegemony of the North Atlantic nations. It
inaugurated the era of nuclear war and the
exploration of space. In 1934 the world was
dominated by colonialism and
industrialization; in 1984 we are preoccupied
with the information explosion and global
consciousness.

The world has become smaller and more
interdependent since 1934. We are
increasingly aware of people and events in
places both near and remote all over the
globe. Places which were once exotic
settings for fabulous stories or childhood
fantasies such as Aladdin and his lamp, Marco
Polo, and Genghis Khan, are now stops on our
regular travels, or at least seem less
fabulous because they are more familiar. The

"mysterious Orient" is as close as our
Panasonic television or Toyota automobile.
"Darkest Africa" is no longer the home of
Tarzan, but an identifiable part of our own
world.

Another difference between our world and
the world of Barmen is increased
diversification. The shrinking of the world
through technological advances in
communication and transportation has brought
its diversity closer to each of us. The
world of our consciousness is no longer
homogenous, but comprises the richness of the
entire planet and its people. Because we are
more aware of global diversity, we are also
more conscious that the way we live and the
things we believe are but one expression of
the diversity within the human community.

Finally, our world differs from the
world of 1933 in that it faces
over-population, nuclear war, and
environmental destruction. What we have
learned from Barmen took place in that past
world; what we have yet to learn must be
expressed in this new context.

As important as these differences are, there is still much to be learned from Barmen; perhaps not so much because we never did learn it, but because we are so prone to forget. Yad Vashem, the Holocaust Memorial in Jerusalem, is the world's most powerful testimony to the horror of the years of the Holocaust. Near the exit is a simple inscription with the words of Baal Shem Tov: "Forgetfulness leads to exile, while remembrance is the secret of redemption." To examine the record of the war years, the Holocaust, and Barmen is to realize that what we have yet to learn must be a recollection of what we dare not forget.

The Significance of Barmen

The 1984 conference on Barmen is the latest in a series. The first International Scholars Conference on the Church Struggle and the Holocaust was convened in Detroit in 1970. Some of the people attending our conference were present at the earlier meeting, and it, like this one, was the product primarily of Franklin Littell and Hubert Locke. The proceedings of that earlier conference were edited by them as

The German Church Struggle and the Holocaust.

Theodore Gill wrote a provocative paper included in the first conference volume, a paper sharply questioning some common assumptions about Barmen.[1] In this paper I propose to respond to Gill.

In essence, Gill questions whether Barmen was, in fact, a constructive step in the struggle for religious freedom and human dignity. Barmen, he reminds us, was predicated on a reaffirmation of the specific responsibilities of Christians to conform their lives to the particularity of the Christian tradition. Gill asks whether this kind of response to political realities, grounded in parochial and exclusive claims of the Christian tradition alone, is sufficient in the modern pluralistic world. He formulated the critical problem clearly: Is the project of achieving universal liberation best grounded in a reaffirmation of the particularity of the Christian tradition, or in affirmation of the natural dignity and freedom of all human beings?

Our reply to this question will determine our understanding of Barmen, establish the course of theology for the next decade, and set the stage for the future of interreligious dialogue and cooperation in the modern world.

The traditional interpretation of Barmen and its significance is clearly stated by Arthur Cochrane in his classic book, The Church's Confession Under Hitler. Cochrane acknowledges that secular historians have paid little attention to the Church struggle. For example, in The Rise and Fall of the Third Reich, William Shirer devotes only seven out of twelve hundred pages to it. Cochrane writes:

> Perhaps it is the nature of the case, however, that secular historians should ignore the Church Struggle. The Church's resistance to Hitlerism, viewed politically and sociologically, did not really amount to very much and had little apparent effect upon the course of events.[2]

Cochrane goes on to say, however, that in spite of this strange neglect by secular historians, the Church Struggle provides a "clue to the deepest cause of the sickness of our age."

During the first part of the twentieth century in Europe, Protestant theology was dominated by humanistic liberalism, rooted in the Enlightenment and intertwined with the Romantic movement. The Enlightenment theology of liberal humanism, articulated by Schleiermacher, was a reaction to the authoritarianism and dogmatism of earlier eighteenth century protestant theology. It was, however, unable to provide a theological or philosophical base for any ethical resistance to Nazism. Liberal humanism was, in fact, responsible for the capitulation of many theologians and humanists to the Third Reich. The Barmen synod, led by Karl Barth, was a radical reversal of theological perspective, turning away from liberal humanism to the neo-orthodox Reformation theology. Neo-orthodox theology, grounded not in the Enlightenment but rather in the Reformation tradition, was able to provide the basis for a Confessing Church's theological opposition to Hitler.

Cochrane and others see liberal humanism itself as a "clue to the deepest cause of the sickness of our age," as a kind of pragmatism that lacks adequate moral and ethical standards. Barmen was significant because it provided an alternative to this Enlightenment theology.

This, roughly, is the interpretation of Barmen that Ted Gill questions. Gill argues that Barmen was not the basis for resistance to totalitarianism and that liberal humanism is the only philosophical alternative to various dogmatisms and despotisms. Gill claims that most of the central figures in the Church Struggle abandoned the position defined by Barmen and returned to liberal humanism before the War was over.

One thing the Confessing Church did show us all. It showed us that in the adult world the church is not big enough anymore by itself to effect much. Dietrich Bonhoeffer found out at last what

his father and brothers had been
telling him since he was fifteen:
the church was not important enough
anymore in the things that matter
most to justify giving his life to
it.[3]

Moreover, Gill argues that the Confessing
Church was too little and too late. Its
leaders did not react to Hitler until well
past the time for alarm. And when it did
react, it was ineffective.

> The Confessing Church was just
> too limited. It influenced some.
> They did not all stick. And all
> together, did they do much? Yes,
> they put one fleeting, drowned
> fragrance in the otherwise
> universal stench. They were a
> winsome bunch; a winsome, crumbling
> bunch.[4]

Gill argues the real leaders of the
resistance were not Confessing Christians, or
even Christians at all; they were "agnostics,
atheists, socialists, communists." And even
those who were Christians (and who were

Confessing Christians)were in many instances
not motivated by the Christocentric theology
presented by Barmen. Gill asserts that they
were, to a great extent, natural theologians
with their roots in liberalism and the
Enlightenment.

All of this leads Gill to his
conclusion that the only real protection
against totalitarianism does not come from
the confessing theology of Barmen, but from
exactly the kind of liberal humanism Barmen
rejected.

> Humanize, humanize, that is
> the ticket: men, their freedom,
> their chances, their creativity,
> their relationships, fulfillments,
> hopes--that is what we keep our eye
> on, whatever or whoever it is that
> aims our vision. It is
> transgressions in these areas that
> give us our warnings.[5]

The first and most significant lesson to
learn from Barmen is that the majority of
well-meaning Christians and other good
citizens loyally supported, or at least

abstained, while the juggernaut of the Third
Reich smashed through all barriers to
barbaric genocide. This complicity of the
"good Christians" must always remain a
warning. Whatever the government or belief,
the demonic temptation to religious
justification of totalitarian oppression is
always present. In Germany in the 1930's,
the cultured supporters of the Third Reich
were educated in the traditions of the
Enlightenment and liberal humanism. Gill
does not tell us, however, how his proposed
return to liberalism could avoid a
repetition of this travesty of Enlightenment
and tragedy of humanism.

Barmen teaches that the liberal humanism
of the Enlightenment was inadequate and had
to be corrected by a particularistic
reaffirmation of Christianity. But as Gill
saw, we have yet to learn in what ways this
corrective is also limited. History does
move on. In Germany in the 1930's it was
essential to reaffirm the particularity of
the Christian tradition. In the United
States in the 1980's that affirmation is still
essential, but not enough. The present
requires neither the reductionism of liberal

humanism, nor the reductionism of theological particularism, but the affirmation of a genuine pluralism recognizing the uniqueness and inviolability of the plurality of human and religious traditions. This affirmation of a new religious pluralism can point the way to a social ethic adequate for the struggle against new styles of totalitarianism in the twenty-first century.

Christianity and the State

Barmen made it clear that the state did not have the right to define what it meant to be Christian. Barmen recognized, and this was crucial, that the religious community precedes, and takes precedence over, the political community in its act of self-definition. In the contemporary world, it is usual to think of political realities as being the fundamental social organizations. Other forms of organizing-- guilds, fraternities, fellowships and churches--take place in the political order. One result of this assumption is that many people in the United States think the state gives the churches certain rights.

This is a shortsighted interpretation of the constitution and is contrary to the insights concerning church and state that informed Barmen. The framers of Barmen saw clearly that they had not to seek redress from the state or to ask it to insure their rights, for the state had no rights in this area. Religious freedom is prior to political organization.

This is an absolutely essential distinction. On this score Barth posed searching questions about the work of Vatican II thirty years after Barmen. Here is what he wrote then:

> When or where did the witnesses in the Old and New Testaments demand a legally assured scope for their life and the proclamation of their faith, and for the presentation of other religions?
> When or where did they defend their freedom to act by reference to the natural dignity of the human person? When or where did they commend this freedom to the

authorities as being in their own best interests?

When or where did they react to the threats of oppression which the ruling powers raised against freedom in any other manner than by resisting and suffering?

Why does the Declaration (except for the final sentence in 15,5) have nothing to say about the true freedom for which the Son makes us free (John 8:36), which is there where the spirit of the Lord is present (2 Cor. 3:17), and nothing about the liberating "law of the Spirit of life in Christ Jesus" (Rom. 8:2), which is itself judgement (James 2:12)? In short, why does it say nothing about "the glorious liberty of the children of God" (Rom. 8:21)? Could not the Church, which is called to this freedom (Gal. 5:13) and stands in it (Gal. 5:1) by speaking to and for itself, have given more powerful testimony to governments and to all mankind about "religious" freedom than it did in this Declaration?[6]

The point is critical. To think that religious liberty is granted by the state is to give the state priority, to make religion secondary. This tends to deify the state. To the contrary, religious liberty precedes the state and and is not granted by the state. The religious community precedes the political community. We, as human beings, are first of all religious and secondarily political.

Barmen teaches us that the Church has certain rights and prerogatives that limit the state. We have yet to learn the ways in which the state's recognition of these rights may be worked out in a religiously plural context. Because the definition of the church affects its relationship to the state, Barmen asked: Was the the German Church or the Confessing Church the "real" church? In this question, the problem of the marks of the church is critical.

In the contemporary religiously plural context, the situation is more complex. The issue is not the relationship of the Church to the state, but the relationship of the

state to religious groups of all sorts. The
definition of religion is more critical and
also more difficult. In a religiously plural
situation, it is no longer adequate to appeal,
as Barmen did, to the freedom in Jesus Christ
as the guarantee of religious freedom for all
groups. We have learned that the religious
community takes priority. What we have yet
to learn is how to identify these communities
in a pluralistic world and how to develop an
adequate theology of religions.

Christianity and Other Religions

Two distinct and apparently
contradictory themes concerning the
relationship of Christianity to other
religions emerge from the Christian
tradition. On the one hand, there is the
clear emphasis on the particularity and
exclusivity of Christianity; on the other
hand, there is a strongly universalist and
tolerant note.

Christian exclusivism has its roots in
the iconoclasm of the Old Testament, as well
as within the New Testament witness to
Jesus as the Christ.[7]

"Everything is entrusted to me by my Father; and no one knows the Son but the Father, and no one knows the Father but the Son and those to whom the Son may choose to reveal him." (Matt. 11:27, Lk. 10:22) "But there are other sheep of mine, not belonging to this fold, whom I must bring in; and they too will listen to my voice. There will then be one flock, one shepherd." (Jn. 10:16) "There is no salvation in anyone else at all, for there is no other name under heaven granted to men, by which we may receive salvation." (Acts 4:12) "They had refused obedience long ago, while God waited patiently in the days of Noah and the building of the ark; and in the ark a few persons, eight in all, were brought to safety through the water. This water prefiguredthe water of baptism through which you are now brought to safety." (1 Pet. 3:20) "Jesus then came up and spoke to them. He said: 'Full

authority in heaven and on earth
has been committed to me. Go forth
therefore and make all nations my
disciples; baptize men everywhere
in the name of the Father and the
Son and the Holy Spirit, and teach
them to observe all that I have
commanded you. And be assured, I
am with you always, to the end of
time.'" (Matt. 28:18-20) "Then he
said to them: 'Go forth to every
part of the world, and proclaim the
Good News to the whole creation.
Those who believe it and receive
baptism will find salvation; those
who do not believe will be
condemned.' " (Mk. 16:15-16)

Cyprian codified these passages into the
classic statement of Christian exclusivism:
"Extra ecclesiam nullus salus est." (Outside
the Church there is no salvation.) Jack
Finnegan describes the modern form of this
mentality as follows:

This tradition led, in course
of time, to a famous and in its own

way beautiful hymn about Greenland's icy mountains and the island of Ceylon where every prospect pleases and only man is vile and heathen because in his blindness he bows down to wood and stone. The hymnist, not quite remembering that this whole planet has many pleasing prospects, forgets that in people found everywhere (such as in Europe during the Holocaust and in the United States with its Hiroshima) one can find vileness of conduct. Not quite remembering either, and possibly not even knowing, that it was on that same island of Sri Lanka that Buddhagbosa wrote his noble <u>Path of Purity</u>.[8]

Christian toleration and inclusivism, on the other hand, is equally well-represented in the sacred texts and the developing doctrinal tradition.

The God of Israel was the same God who also inspired prophets among the heathen: God's grace

reached to Job the Uzzite, Balaam
the Syrian, and Melchizedek the
Canaanite. In the Gospels, one of
the few areas in which we can see
spiritual growth in Jesus is his
increasing awareness of the
acceptability of non-Israelites:
He gained positive regard for the
Syro-Phonecian woman on account of
her persistence (Mk. 7:24-30); he
reversed his "limited commission,"
in which he forbade his disciples
to announce the rule of God among
the Gentiles, and sent them instead
to tell the Good News to all
"nations." (Mt. 10:5-7; 28:19).
In the parable of the Good
Samaritan (Lk. 10:29-37), Jesus
taught that anyone who shows
kindness is "a neighbor,"
regardless of racial, cultural, or
religious identity. He generalized
this attitudinal openness in the
"great commandment" when he
explained that loving your neighbor
as you love yourself is as
important as loving God. (Mk.
12:29-32) And when his disciples

demonstrated the beginnings of religious exclusiveness against someone whom they refused to acknowledge religiously, Jesus chided them: "Whoever is not against you is on your side." (Lk. 9:49-50)

This openness of Christianity to God's revelation among other religious communities was demonstrated in the traditional stories of Jesus' birth. The Chaldean astrologers gazed at their horoscopes and followed the stars to find the fulfillment of their astrological and Zoroastrian hopes in Bethlehem. (Matt. 2:1-12)

When Paul and Barnabas reached Lystra, and the pagans there greeted them as if they were gods, it became part of their missionary method to acknowledge that God "has not left the gentiles without some clue to his nature." (Acts 14:17) And at Athens, the Apostle to the Gentiles accorded some Greek poets with the same status as inspired Old Testament prophets, quoting them as proof-texts in his sermon to the philosophers. (Acts 17:28-29)

Justin the Martyr combined these
motivations with his understanding of the
Creator Logos mentioned in John, chapter one,
and codified the theological inclusivist
attitude in his Logos Christology. The
Logos Spermatikos, said Justin, is the
divine Word of the Father, sown like seed
everywhere in the field of the world,
scattered in the soil of human thought. The
Fathers of the Eastern Church followed
Justin's lead and were not ashamed to extend
their religious fellowships to Plato,
Socrates, and Aristotle, whom they called
"Christians before Christ."

Both these themes within the Christian
tradition find expression in Barmen. On the
one hand, Jesus Christ alone is acknowledged
to be Lord, a strong affirmation of the
tradition of Christian exclusivism, which
continued to find articulation in the
theological conservatism that followed
Barmen. On the other hand, the importance of
Judaism was a critical issue. Although a
pro-Jewish affirmation did not emerge
explicitly in the Barmen declaration, Barth
wrote to Eberhard Bethge much later:

It was new to me that
Bonhoeffer (as I read your biography
of him) in 1933 viewed the Jewish
problem as the first and decisive
question, even as the only one, and
took it in hand so energetically.
I myself have long felt guilty that
I did not make this problem
central, at least public, in the
two Barmen declarations of 1934
which I had composed. In 1934,
certainly, a text in which I said a
word to that effect would not have
found agreement either in the
Reformed Synod of January 1934 or
in the General Synod of May at
Barmen-- if one considers the
state of mind of the confessors of
faith in those days. But that I
was caught up in my own affairs
somewhere else is no excuse for my
not having properly fought for this
cause.[9]

It is not incidental that the horrors of
the Holocaust focus on a religious issue.
Its victims were a particular people, a

people identified by their ethnic and
religious heritage. The Holocaust was not
visited on a random part of the population,
but on this concrete community. This means
that the persecution and survival of the Jews
is a Christian concern.

The frenetic effort to
reconstruct artificially a
religious monolith after the gods
have died--whether that monolith be
the "German faith" or "Christian
America" or Islam--invariably leads
from hatred of the Jews to overt
forms of attack.

For those who will join me in
repudiation of religion-in-general
and spirituality without content or
integrity, but who are not prepared
to use the Christian theological
formulation, let me state it thus:
we are so situated in our various
national and racial contexts that
we cannot in fact love humanity
without loving concrete, earthy,
historic persons and groups. Under
pressure, we shall either
retrogress to our first love of the

Gentile tribe or nation, or we shall love that Israel whose prophets and seers point us toward a day of universal justice and righteousness, mercy and peace. Hatred of the Jews is often the first seismographic reading of the covert emergence of a false particularism, and we must learn to recognize it as such.[10]

What can be learned about contemporary religious pluralism from this discussion of the responsibility of Christians, as Christians, for Judaism? Certainly Judaism bears an historical relationship to Christianity significantly different from other religions. Christianity arose out of Judaism. They share a common history that is longer than their independent histories. They share common holy ground, common scriptures, and common symbols. They worship the same God. This unique relationship of Christianity to Judaism must not be overlooked. But, the relation of Christianity to Judaism is also analogous to the relationship of Christianity to other religions: Judaism and Christianity are

different religions and form distinct and
different religious communities.

Religious pluralism and the appropriate
attitude of Christians toward other religions
is an insufficiently explored and expressed
issue within the Christian tradition.
Christians, as well as Jews and Muslims, have
much to learn about the morality of this
issue from Eastern religions. We have yet to
learn how to honor the uniqueness of the
various religious traditions and enhance the
common interest they share.

Christianity and Natural Theology

There is a theology implicit in the
Third Reich and Mein Kampf. Nazism was, in
one way or another, a religious movement.
The symbols, rituals, ceremonies, language
and songs, and even hatreds and fears,
motivated and used the religious
consciousness and sensibilities of people.
Barth wrote:

> National Socialism, according
> to its own revelation of what it
> is--a self-revelation to which it

has devoted all the time and chance
till now allowed--is as well
without any doubt something quite
different from a political
experiment. It is, namely, a
<u>religious institution of
salvation</u>.[11]

The success of National Socialism during
the thirties lay in its effectivenes in
filling the religious vacuum that existed in
Europe at that time. The religious vacuum
was in part created by the natural theology
that was associated with the Enlightenment.
Natural theology denied the existential
dimension to faith, for it operated in the
intellectual mode and attempted to root faith
in reflective validation. Neglect of the
emotional, mystical side of the religious
life, embodied in particular religious
traditions, left the way wide open for Nazism
to come into that dimension with its demonic
forces.

For the Confessing Church, the conflict was
between a natural theology rooted in race
and faith rooted in the particular tradition
of Christianity. Since natural theology

appears to many people to be the basis for understanding between Christians and non-Christians, conflict between the theology associated with Barmen and the demands of religious toleration and cooperation becomes acute.

Karl Barth worked out most fully the theological rejection of natural theology.[12]   As he saw it, natural theology is a way of avoiding the risk and commitment of faith. In nineteenth century liberalism, natural theology assumed a humanistic premise that undercut the uniqueness of the Christian tradition. (And, one might say in anticipation, also undercut the uniqueness of any religious tradition.) Barth's "Copernican Revolution" in theology halted the synergistic tendencies of Enlightenment theology and focused on the uniqueness of the Christian tradition.

It has sometimes been assumed that Barth's "confessionalism" makes theology safe. If theology is not in a position to accept a common ground with philosophy, for example, then there can be no arguments for or against it. If theology is based solely on revelation and if the theologian has that revelation, then he is secure from all attack. This is to miss Barth's point by exactly 180 degrees. The real intention of Barth's position intensifies the risk for the theologian. Theology is no longer merely an intellectual risk, but an existential risk also. Barth demands that the theologian express himself in terms of what he understands, that he put himself and his thought on the line, open to criticism and attack.

Barth's rejection of natural theology is a rejection of "belief." "Belief" is one's ascription to a set of <u>propositions</u>. This is what natural theology is about. Natural theology does not involve commitment. It involves assent. The difference between mental assent and existential commitment is all the difference in the world. Genuine theology is the voice of the committed seeker after truth.

We cannot experiment with unbelief, even if we think we know and possess all sorts of interesting and very promising possibilities and recipes for it.... But faith itself--or rather, the real God in whom faith believes--must be taken so seriously that there is not place at all for even an apparent transposition to the standpoint of unbelief, or the pedagogic and playful self-lowering into the sphere of its possibilities. When faith takes itself seriously, who has peace or freedom for this apparent assimilation into this game with unbelief? Who is it who really has to stoop down at this point? Not one man to another, a believer to an unbeliever, as all natural theology fatally but inevitably supposes. He who stoops down to the level of us all, both believers and unbelievers, is the real God alone, in His grace and mercy. And it is only by the fact that he knows this that the believing man is distinguished from the unbeliever. Faith consists precisely in this, in the life which is lived in consequence of God's coming down to our level. But if this is faith, and the knowledge of faith is the knowledge of this, the believing man is the one who will find unbelief first and foremost in himself. First and foremost he will find only unbelief in himself; enmity against the truth and deprivation of the truth. How, then, can he have place and freedom to descend to the level of other men, to play that game with unbelief?[14]

Natural theology is, then, an escape from commitment, and because of that it is an escape from genuine dialogue and meeting. It is the basis for disinterested speculation, not for committed dialogue. The failure of the Enlightenment legacy was that Enlightenment rationality left us with a discursive and dispassionate debate, but not with a language of commitment. The trust of Barmen was to reintroduce that note into the language of the Church.

What we have yet to learn is how to translate this realization from the

Christian, European context in which it was formulated into the context of the entire world, the world's religions and the world theologies now emerging. We need not just confessional Christian theologies but a world theology, built not on natural theology, but one built on pluralism. We have yet to learn how to meet each other in the religiously plural world and how to acknowledge, in genuine openness, all the traditions and backgrounds out of which humanity has come.

Christianity and Culture

The horrors of 1934 were due in part, to a cultural chauvinism that identified the existing culture with Christianity. The Nazi's used religion to validate and legitimize their totalistic political regime. It was just this kind of legitimization and validation that Barmen rejected.

National Socialism represented the ultimate in the identification of religion with culture. There was no distinction; the history of its culture was the history of its religion. This provided an integration of society and a cohesion of the individual and society that gave National Socialism its totalitarian unity. Opposing this religious-cultural homogeniety, Barmen emphasized the difference between the religious tradition of Christianity and the cultural tradition of the German people. For Barmen, Christianity stood as a critical check and challenge to cultural imperialism. The Third Reich achieved its power, in part, through the religious validation of secular power. Barmen sought to counter by asserting that Christianity could not be identified with any particular cultural tradition.

This is the point at which Barth had so much trouble with liberal theologians like Reinhold Niebuhr.[15] Barth insisted that the Church should not identify itself with particular political causes, but should stand apart from partisan politics; that the issue should be joined by the Confessing church not as a humanitarian cause, but as a religious, Christian cause. The cause the church had to champion was not human rights, but the freedom of the gospel.

The problem with this position from the perspective of other countries and other cultures is that the Confessing Church was as culturally determined as the German Church. From this larger perspective, Barmen represents merely another--if more benign-- form of cultural chauvinism. This, I believe, is the point Theodore Gill makes.

We have learned from Barmen and Barth, however, that a return to the Enlightenment theology proposed by Gill is inadequate. The natural theology and humanism he proposes is just as chauvinistic as any particular confessional tradition. Most important, it has no way of successfully avoiding the identification of religion with culture that was characteristic of the German tragedy.

We have yet to learn how to formulate a theology that recognizes the cultural limitations of every religious expression but uses that as an opportunity for learning and growth. The way out of the cultural chauvinism that produced the Holocaust is neither through a return to liberal humanism nor though entrenchment in the theology of Barmen, but an advance to the next stage of

religious pluralism. Peter Berger expressed
it this way:

> What then is the form of
> interreligious dialogue that I
> think we should strive for? I
> think it is the common search for
> truth by people who are not safely
> grounded in any tradition. I want
> to emphasize the "common" and
> "truth" of what I've said: a
> common search for truth.
>
> The "common" is, I think, very
> much implied in my sociological
> analysis of the situation. It has
> to be common because we are more or
> less in the same boat--all of us.
> It's the opposite of what might be
> called "diplomatic negotiation":
> "I represent this, you represent
> that..."
>
> Represent? I don't
> represent anything. I represent
> myself with my own uncertainties
> and that's what I bring into the
> situation. Most of us are in this
> boat. The ones who are not,
> frankly, are not very useful,

except as informants. They can
tell us what the tradition is which
they believe so firmly. Well,
thank you, now we know! But in
terms of the common quest that is
the task that I see, I don't find
people like that terribly helpful.
It is the uncertain ones, the
doubting ones, the people who want
to find out where they are--there,
I think, is where the most
productive work will be done.

But also terribly important is
the search for <u>truth</u>. If one
takes this business seriously, I
think one can not be satisfied by
phenomenology or by our endlessly
evolving sophisticated
understandings of the other
possibilities of religious faith
that are available to us in our
situation. Sooner or later one
must ask: "Okay, I now understand
as much as I can, as much as I want
to at this point, in terms of all
the background on this. <u>Where do
I stand on it?</u>"[16]

Berger foreshadows a new spirit of pluralism, rooted in the religious quest and in an appreciation of the uniqueness and necessity of particular religious traditions, that moves beyond both the liberal humanism represented by Gill and the confessionalism of Barmen.

Conclusion

Barmen marks a critical turning point in the history of Western religious thought. It moves away from the theology of the Enlightenment which was the culmination of the Western intellectual tradition inherited from Greece and Rome. At the same time, Barmen was a rediscovery of a particular, concrete tradition and an existential dimension in religious life and thought. It was a rejection of the detachment, rationalism, and cultural myopia of liberal thought and a return to the deeper religious truths embodied in the positive tradition of Christianity.

Now it is necessary to take the next step and translate this rediscovery of particularity into a world-wide perspective.

We have to learn how to move beyond this realization in our political and social context of religious pluralism to an affirmation of the common and collective spiritual journey of all human beings. Through religious pluralism and global vision we can move beyond both the Enlightenment and Barmen into a new phase of theological and religious vitality.

Footnotes

1. Gill, Theodore A., "What Can America Learn from the German Church Struggle?" The German Church Struggle and the Holocaust, Franklin H. Littell and Hubert G. Locke (eds.), (Detroit: Wayne State University Press, 1974), pp. 278-290.

2. Cochrane, Arthur C., The Church's Confession Under Hitler, Second Edition (Pittsburg: Pickwick Press, 1976), p. 12.

3. Gill, loc. cit., p. 285.

4. Ibid.

5. Ibid., p. 286.

6. Cochrane, Arthur C., "The Message of Barmen for Contemporary Church History," Littell and Locke, p. 192.

7. Finnegan, Jack, "Biblical Sources for Christian Attitudes Toward Other Religions," The New Ecumenical Research Association Conference on World Theology, San Francisco, April, 1982. Unpublished paper.

8. Ibid.

9. Bethge, Eberhard, "Troubled Self-Interpretation and Uncertain

Reception in the Church Struggle,"
Littell and Locke, op. cit., p. 167.

10. Littell, Franklin, "Church Struggle and
    the Holocaust," Littell and Locke, op.
    cit., p. 18.

11. Littell and Locke, op. cit., pp.
    41-43.

12. Bettis, Joseph, "Theology in the Public
    Debate: Barth's Rejection of Natural
    Theology and the Hermeneutical Problem,"
    Scottish Journal of Theology, Vol. 22,
    No. 4, (Dec. 1969), pp. 385-403.

13. Barth, Karl Church Dogmatics, 11/1,
    p. 246f.

14. Ibid., p. 95.

15. Bettis, Joseph, "Theology and Politics:
    Karl Barth and Reinhold Niebuhr on
    Social Ethics After Liberalism,"
    Religion in Life, Vol. XLVII, No. 1
    (Spring, 1979), pp. 53-62.

16. Berger, Peter, "The Pluralistic
    Situation and the Coming Dialogue
    Between the World Religions,"
    Buddhist-Christian Studies, Vol. 1,
    1981, p. 39.

RELIGION, TOTALITARIANISM, AND HUMAN FREEDOM: REFLECTIONS ON BARMEN

- Lyman H. Legters

In 1921 a young student from Berlin, grown weary of his Heidelberg dissertation, took time out and wrote a novel. The manuscript lay in his drawer for several years until a colleague from the famous Vossische Zeitung of Berlin drew it to the attention of the publisher, S. Fischer Verlag, whereupon it was published, in 1927, under the title, Torstenson: Entstehung einer Diktatur (Torstenson: the Rise of a Dictatorship). For this first literary effort, the author, Hans Meisel, received the Kleist prize in that same year. The book's success with the reading public did not equal its critical acclaim, partly no doubt because it was presently overtaken by the rise of an all too real dictatorship, one that also overtook the author and caused him to leave Germany in 1934.

The fictional dictatorship of the novel arises in the Baltic region amidst the political chaos afflicting that part of the world in the aftermath of World War I and the Russian Revolution. Torstenson, a coolly manipulative general of Swedish origin, makes himself irreplaceable in that cauldron of ethnic, national, and class conflict, gradually drawing unto himself the threads of political maneuver and decision-making until, all other forces having been defeated or discredited, he is the de facto dictator of the small country on the Baltic. The novel is a brilliant account of the persons and forces that figured in Torstenson's success, a compelling anatomization of a political process which, while far from exceptional even when Meisel wrote his novel, has since become depressingly common throughout the world.

When the novel was reissued by Fischer Verlag in 1971[1], it was accompanied by an epilogue by the author, by then retired after a distinguished professorial career at the University of Michigan. In the new epilogue, Meisel deflated the tendency to see his fictional work as some kind of prefiguring of the Nazi dictatorship. He pointed out that it would have been quite impossible at the time of writing to anticipate the singular features of Hitlerism, noting that his Torstenson had more in common with a figure like General von Schleicher, the last pre-Nazi German chancellor, or even with General de Gaulle in a time closer to our own, than to Hitler. What he had created fictionally was an unmasking, a laying-bare, of the essentially modern political maneuvering that has, over and over again, favored the emergence of military or crypto-military dictatorship as a rational counterforce to chaos and anarchy, or as a remedy for what may appear from time to time in ordinary political life as an intolerable level of uncertainty.

His work had been and, although insufficiently noticed, continued to be a remarkable exercise in what its author was subsequently to call "political science fiction," the use of novelistic form to display with great acuity fundamental political process in this instance the process that ensues when civic responsibility and the bonds of political community are unequal to the forces of disorder -- when the egoism of ambitious leadership overrides the rule of law and the guarantees that we, especially in the Anglo-American world, take for granted as constitutional proscriptions. But for the intrusion of Hitlerism and Stalinism (also unimaginable at the time of writing), Meisel's Torstenson might even have registered as a prophetic piece of fiction, given the frequency with which the modern world has had resort to similar antidotes to disorder. Hitler and Stalin succeeded, however, in rendering the novel tame, almost acceptably ordinary, just because their unexampled tyrannies so far surpassed the mere phenomenon of a manipulative dictatorship filling the vacuum left by the interplay of incompatible and intransigent forces in a political arena that is up for grabs. Certainly the failure to prefigure what we have since learned to call

totalitarianism is no reproach to the novel
or its author; such an accomplishment would
have counted, at the time, as belonging to
the utopian (better: dystopian) genre, quite
a different kind of imaginative exercise.
What makes Torstenson germane to the
present topic, in any case, is precisely the
contrast between its depiction of ordinary
political process issuing in ordinary
military dictatorship and the unusual, indeed
quite extraordinary, quality that appeared in
twin configurations a few years after the
novel's first appearance to disqualify it as
political prophecy. I refer, of course, to
Hitlerism and Stalinism, those peculiar 20th
century excrescences that gave rise to the
notion of totalitarianism.

There are, it seems to me, two salient
features of Meisel's brilliant portrayal that
can be extracted from his interwar European
world (in which they are counterposed to each
other) and applied precisely to the
subsequent developments that now make that
political world seem incredibly remote. One
is simply popular religious fervor; the
other, what we may, following Jürgen

Habermas and other contemporary social theorists, term instrumental rationality.[2]

The latter quality, familiarly associated since Weber's pioneering studies with bureaucracy in general,[3] is simply a cool and detached calculus of strategy, a reckoning of the means necessary to the attainment of preordained goals, unconstrained by any overriding normative principles or ethical prohibitions. Instrumental rationality seldom entails needless brutality and may at times even register as an antidote to arbitrary cruelty.[4] Although it usually resists the fixing of responsibility and strict accountability (except to the next higher level of its hierarchy), it takes pride in adherence to rules that are mostly public and not arcane; and it is generally efficient, notwithstanding the popular image of bureaucracy, in relating the expenditure of means to the anticipated difficulty of reaching an assigned objective. It does not shrink from adopting inhuman means when necessary--it is indeed the plenitude and potency of technique available to instrumental rationality in the modern world

that makes it so frightening--but its pride
and joy is the efficient matching of means
and assigned outcome. In the political world
of Meisel's Torstenson, instrumental
rationality is sufficient. Since the goal is
an ambitious one, the techniques employed may
sometimes be drastic but should not be
excessive; they may be immoral but should not
be fiendish.

The former quality, what I have called
popular religious fervor,[5] figures in the
novel as the only real threat to the
dictator's calculations. Resembling
chiliastic and millennarian religious
movements of medieval Europe or the
revivalism of the American frontier, a mass
upsurge of Russian peasants--that
unaccountably stops short of Torstenson's
domain--is clearly the one kind of force that
eludes the dictator's rational calculation
and therefore threatens the edifice he has
constructed. No confrontation is needed to
account for Torstenson's uneasiness, for just
the rumor of a primitive and irrational force
moving in his direction has been enough to
exhibit the limitations of his maneuvering

and manipulation, of an instrumentally
rational dictatorship.

* * * * * * *

The term "totalitarianism" entered our
political vocabulary in the context of the
cold war as scholars and intellectuals
responded to twin shocks. The first shock,
which overtook most people only gradually,
was the sheer enormity of the evils
perpetrated by Hitler's regime. Those who
liberated the death camps knew immediately,
and enough information was available that
anyone could have known, yet the realization
of the Holocaust and associated crimes took
some time to sink into our consciousness.
And as it did so we became aware, prompted by
the emergence of hostility of global
dimensions between the wartime allies, that
villainy of a comparable scope had been
abroad in the world of Stalin. The second
shock was composed of the breakdown of a
wartime alliance on which hopes had been
built and of the recognition, also long
available to those who wished to know but now
useful as well in the arsenal of official
anticommunism,[6] that Stalin's personal

dictatorship could vie with Hitler's in the catalogue of modern political reprehensibility. These twin shocks reverberated in the form of a new coinage in our political language: totalitarianism.

Interwar Germany had in fact produced some foreshadowings in expressions such as "total power" (totale Macht) and "total mobilization" (totale Mobilmachung), the adjectival addition serving to hint even then at a distinctively modern political phenomenon, an unprecedented technical capability wielded in some cause that overrides all constraints. (Lest we become complacent about these things that happen in other places, it is well to remember that the terms and the technical capabilities they call to mind are perfectly fitting for the conduct of World War II by members, ourselves included, of the western alliance.) At any rate, by the time postwar West Germany reentered the world of western political discourse, the expression "totalitarianism" had been invented and was taken over into German (Totalitarismus; adjectivally, totalitär) in its new English meaning, thus supplanting in a curious manner its own terminological antecedents.[7] Because the western world has since talked of totalitarianism as if it were something real, a genuine phenomenon, it may be well to recall the purpose for which the expression was designed.

It was the realization that, despite ideological and military antipathy (except for the two years of the Molotov-Ribbentrop Pact), Hitlerism and Stalinism exhibited certain common yet unprecedented features, that urged the need for a new term. "Tyranny" and "despotism," fitting as far as they went, were somehow inadequate to convey the unexampled capabilities available to the ruler of a powerful modern state; suggesting examples throughout human history, such terms failed to capture the singularities of twentieth century experience with personal dictatorship. The addition of "modern" to "dictatorship" might have sufficed if all that was needed was to suggest the technological plenitude available to contemporary rulers, but that would not have separated Hitler and Stalin, on the one hand, from the world's Torstensons, or even from wartime presidents and prime ministers, on

the other. The result, without reviewing
here all of the steps in its evolution, was
the germ of a new concept. Totalitarianism
was tailored specifically to capture those
special qualities that made, or seemed to
make, Hitlerism and Stalinism both similar to
each other and, taken together, unique in
relation to all previous or contemporary
forms of autocratic rule.

There are of course certain problems
associated with this intellectual procedure.
The first resides in the foreshortening of
historical perspective: the very nearness in
time of these two experiences coupled with
the trauma they brought to much of the world
may induce us to exaggerate their
distinctiveness. The second arises out of
the narrow range of experience caught within
the net of the newly invented concept:
admitting the unwieldiness of simply piling
up adjectives to convey the special features
of the dictatorships in question, it will
always be open to doubt that two cases
suffice to justify the introduction of a new
term into our political vocabulary. The
third problem in this connection concerns the
trade-off, in the employment of conceptual

and analytical tools, between capturing similarity and preserving distinctions: a concept that focuses entirely on the likenesses between Hitlerism and Stalinism may prove too costly if it obscures equally important dissimilarities. And the fourth, not really intrinsic to the process of validating a new conceptual tool, is the ubiquitous tendency toward debasement of language: a term that implicitly praises or condemns the object to which it is applied is all too readily available for more general rhetorical purposes and may, in general usage, become so diluted that it hinders rather than helps in serious analysis.

My answers to these possible objections, for what they may be worth, are as follows:

1) Although I do not discount the value of historical perspective in understanding singular occurrences, political analysis, especially the kind that seeks to identify and hence avoid catastrophic propensities, is all but useless if it must wait upon that detachment which also entails forgetfulness, that is, the loss of any sense of urgency. Contemporary history is always aware that it

may be carried away by the drama of the immediate but accepts that liability for the sake of addressing actualities that still haunt the present. And, while I think that the cold war supplied a potentially distorting framework for the initial exercises in developing a concept of totalitarianism, we must not forget either that Stalinism posed a very genuine threat in those postwar years, at least to the Soviet people and their nearest neighbors.[8] In that sense, the cold war view had an urgent validity then that has not always been preserved by the softening effect of remoteness and detachment.

2) I admit the preciousness of a political language that must have a special concept for each two or three occurrences that resemble each other (this is one of the things we mean by "jargon"). Furthermore, as a historian, I prefer "old" nomenclature so long as it fits with reasonable precision. Yet I also defend as entirely legitimate the attempt to impart conceptual focus to such conspicuously devastating assaults on human and civilized values, and indeed on human

life itself, as were embodied in Hitlerism
and Stalinism.

3) But it is not equally plain, at
least to me, that in the particular matters
at hand a term like "totalitarianism,"
dwelling as it does on likeness at the
expense of distinctions, does not lose more
than it gains. Both of the twentieth century
dictatorships under examination
unquestionably displayed peculiarly
threatening features. To the degree that
"totalitarianism" captures them rather
exactly, that is, in a way that assists us to
identify possible recurrences in good time,
then, as I have said, the conceptual exercise
is wholly legitimate. But if the term
obscures crucial differences, let us say
between ideological postures or means of
social mobilization, it could impede rather
than enhance the clarification that must
underlie preventive measures in the future.
Given that we are dealing with only two
cases, I would say that the justification for
the new concept is at its weakest at this
point.

4) It must be obvious that those responsible for terminological innovation--for example, Carl J. Friedrich and Hannah Arendt in this instance[9]--cannot be held to account for the abuses that others bestow on their proposed concepts. Examples of debased language abound. "Imperialism" once had a rather definite Marxian content, but what it means these days, in the mouths of Soviet spokespersons, is mainly just disapproval. "Revisionism" is another label that once had historically concrete and logically specifiable meaning, but is now, for the most part, only an in-house epithet in the Soviet realm. Just so, when a secretary of state counterposes "authoritarian" to "totalitarian," the only plausible translation reads: "dictators we like" and "dictators we don't like." Debasement is deplorable, but its likelihood ought not to inhibit our efforts at clarification, including, where warranted, the invention of new terms.

The really serious objections to the concept of totalitarianism are not these general procedural ones, however, but, to my mind at any rate, quite specific ones arising out of the manner in which this particular problem was addressed. One major flaw in the process of defining totalitarianism was the artificiality of enumerating the shared traits of the dictatorships in question.[10] If one is quite sure at the outset that Hitlerism and Stalinism are the exemplary cases, the common traits chosen as defining (not individually, be it noted, but in their collective import) are almost certain to exclude all other existing cases that might be candidates for inclusion and, still more serious, are likely to result in ignoring traits of one or another that are at least equally salient in explaining its horrifying capabilities. To cite just one illustration, it might be thought that a strongly developed tradition of "the rule of law" would be an impediment to (and a weakly developed one an enhancement of) any propensity for a style of rule that we might want to call totalitarian. Germany and Russia stand in rather obvious contrast to each other on this point (that is to say, this is not a shared trait) and the difference may cut in quite opposite directions if one seeks, for example, to account for the relative absence of effective

resistance to both of these dictatorial
regimes.

If, on the other hand, one is not quite
sure that the phenomenon of totalitarianism
is confined to the two cases under
examination, then the traits will likely be
more loosely specified so that additional
cases can be made to fit the definition
irrespective of merely local or accidental
deviations from the model. Then we have
endless debates as to the status of
Mussolini's Italy or a particular
client-state of the Soviet Union. All of
that is, of course, an acceptable part of
working up or working out a definition, and
so long as the debate remains serious a
flexible definition is certainly not to be
deplored. But the process reaches absurdity
when, as happened in the post-Stalin era, we
preserve the label while subtracting one or
more of the defining traits and speak of
"Stalinism without terror" as a continuation
of totalitarian rule. That, of course,
encourages the debasement that works against
clarification and may help to explain how we
reached the point where, as is demonstrably
true in everyday political discourse, even

the guardians of precision employ
"totalitarian" in a thoughtless and even
promiscuous manner. It entails, among other
things, a "slide" from treating the traits
remaining after the subtraction as <u>necessary</u>
to treating them as <u>necessary and
sufficient</u> --the same kind of terminological
sloppiness that sees a genocide in every
deprivation, a Holocaust in every murderous
act.

The other major flaw in the discussion
of totalitarianism--with us now for at least
a generation--has to do with its almost
exclusive emphasis on the finished product:
totalitarian rule. The identification of
totalitarian predispositions or inclinations,
whether in a social movement seeking power or
in a potential ruler, is admittedly a much
thornier problem for the analyst than the
already problematical task of identifying
those salient features of a regime in power
that make it at least presumptively
totalitarian. It is therefore understandable,
at least, that reflection on the problem has
confined itself so largely to totalitarianism
as a system for wielding power and performing
the functions of governance. Yet one of the

things we know with greatest certainty from
the empirical study of Hitlerism and
Stalinism is that effective resistance must
precede the consolidation of power. If these
two regimes represent totalitarianism par
excellence, then it can be said with a high
degree of probability that active resistance
equals martyrdom. And while the world has
not lacked for willing martyrs in some
significant numbers at all stages in human
history, it is not usually to be counted as a
socially pertinent action, i.e., efficacious,
to recommend martyrdom as a form of
opposition.[11] And it seems then to follow
that the practically valuable aspect of the
analysis of totalitarianism could only be a
set of recommendations for prophylaxis. That
dictates a shift to the identification of
totalitarian potentialities.

There is, of course, something else we
know, or ought at least to recognize as
probable, about the phenomenon of
totalitarianism--so far as we fancy that we
have experienced it in recent history--and
this again is something that has received
astonishingly little attention in the
discussion since Hitler's last days and since

the death of Stalin. I refer to the
fragility of such systems of rule, the short
life span of these intensifications of
tyranny that seem, notwithstanding their
claims to permanence, incapable of
institutionalizing whatever it is that makes
them more, or worse, than ordinary autocracy.
The factor that comes first to mind is
naturally the mortality of the personal
dictator, though I would caution against any
assumption that predicated the choice between
action and inaction on either assassination
or geriatric considerations. Although both
totalitarianisms (understood in the sense of
satisfying all the criteria) collapsed when
their architect disappeared, it may be safer
to assume that the problem of succession
could be resolved in some future
manifestation of like tendency.
Nevertheless, whether the delicate balance of
a totalitarian system is viewed as a function
of personal charisma or some kind of
evanescent chemistry of key elements in
workable combination, there is a strong
likelihood that the combined features that
make totalitarianism special will be unable
to survive the regularization or
institutionalization that would, by

definition, be a prerequisite of real durability.

If the foregoing is substantially correct, we are left with the choice of resisting in timely fashion or waiting it out. We know what horrors can be perpetrated in a short time if we choose the latter course, and we do not yet know how to recognize the next threat (unless we mistakenly assume, like the generals of a universal bad joke, that the next war will reenact the last one). What seems to be wanting, then, is a means of identifying totalitarianism in tendency: recognizing one in full bloom may be a worthy intellectual exercise; but only early diagnosis, the anticipation of catastrophe, can aid in its prevention.

* * * * * * * *

If my remarks thus far seem to paint the discussion of totalitarianism into a corner, I would propose, as a way out, a somewhat different approach to the question of definition. Instead of the usual technique of identifying either sets of traits or

historical sequences that culminate in
phenomena (Hitlerism, Stalinism) sufficiently
singular to warrant new terminology, my
suggestion, admittedly sacrificing some
descriptive adequacy to a sharpening of
focus, would be to search for a single
quality that sets them apart from all
ordinary autocracies or despotisms.

The problem with historical sequences,
such as the trajectory of antisemitic thought
and action traced by Hannah Arendt in the
opening section of her study of
totalitarianism, is that they are
indeterminate and open-ended. A rising tide
of antisemitism may certainly help us to
understand the setting in which a Hitler
appears and succeeds, but a Hitler is in no
way a necessary or predictable outcome. We
may agree that such a rising tide, whether in
Germany, the Soviet Union, or anywhere, is
threatening and requires counteraction. But
we "know" of its totalitarian potential
either on the dubious footing that it
happened once before or by waiting to see.
The corresponding difficulty with lists of
traits, such as those enumerated by Friedrich
and Brzezinski,[12] is that they are

descriptively derived from two completed
instances and must recur in recognizably
similar combination before we can add another
instance to the inventory of known
totalitarianisms; they thus take no account
of the possibility (one could even say
likelihood) that the next instance meriting
the designation will find other ways of
achieving its devastation and thus exhibit a
different set of traits.

The singular feature we might seek
instead would, of course, have to be a
quality that both Hitlerism and Stalinism
possessed in unmistakable degree, and
preferably also one that was readily
discernible in the movement or personality
that emerged as a seeker after power before
that power was actually secured. Such a
quality would certainly not be the only
significant emblem of what we may still want
to call totalitarianism; but it would, at
least arguably, be an unfailing identifier of
the tendency that culminates in
totalitarianism and a consistent attribute of
those totalitarian tendencies that reach
fruition by seizing power. In this sense,
then, it would constitute both a necessary

and a sufficient condition for the purpose of identifying totalitarian dispositions and for separating totalitarian systems from mere dictatorships and other autocratic forms.

My candidate for this weighty status as singular identifier is the urge or impulse, easily discoverable in both movements and individual power seekers, toward exaction of willing and even cheerful obedience. This quality reminds us perhaps of an Orwellian notion, utopian or dystopian, of programming people's minds; in effect, securing their complicity in the scheme that controls them. Lest this suggest something unreal or merely fanciful, it is well to remember that both Hitlerism and Stalinism displayed great uneasiness, sometimes characterized as paranoia, about the need to enforce obedience. There was always the supposition that the regime's programs and plans should be received by the citizenry as self-evidently wise and automatically normative. Thus, while there was no reluctance to enforce obedience in either case (true of any tyranny or dictatorship), what was sought was an automatic or self-enforcing mechanism within the populace

that would remove the need for coercion.
Sometimes we call this thought control.

Parenthetically, it may be useful to
point to the real-world model for this sort
of thing that, if achieved on a societal
scale, we could call a perfected
totalitarianism: the miniature version is
the mental asylum, not because it is
necessarily vicious or malevolent but because
its inmates (citizens) are automatically
disqualified by their status as patients from
the exercise of judgment. Proximate order is
assured by the immunity of the professional
staff (government) from criticism or
correction by their constituents. And an
ideal order is in sight when the clients
concur in their own disqualification and
concede that the ruling experts know what is
best for all concerned.[13]

This urge to control thought and belief
on a societal scale seems to me to be the
only item from the familiar lists of traits
and the only one of the climaxes of
historical sequences that does not occur
rather commonly in other circumstances,
historical and contemporary, that we would

<u>not</u> be inclined to classify with Hitlerism
and Stalinism as uniquely devastating to the
peoples who fall under their sway. Of
course, we might expect other threatening
dispositions to appear in combination with
this urge to control the minds of citizens,
but, despite the hint of circularity in my
argument, I submit that this is the only
feature of the two recent historical
experiences that decisively marks them off
from what we know of autocracy in general,
whether of an autocratic system in power or
of the autocratic character of some political
movements.

It may help to make the argument more
substantial at this point to return to Hans
Meisel's <u>Torstenson</u>, recalling that the
rational maneuvers of the dictator were there
counterposed to a spontaneous mass movement
animated by religious fervor. It was exactly
that counterposition that made the novel such
a taut and realistic depiction of political
process and, at the same time, disqualified
it as pre-Hitlerian prophecy. To put it
differently, it was Hitlerism that broke the
mold of realistic politics, in fact nullified
politics as commonly understood, by an

innovation that was replicated, in other ways and for different reasons, by Stalinism. The innovation was the joining of coldly rational machinery of governance and popular fervor of recognizably religious intensity.

A few qualifications may be advisable here to meet some obvious objections. These two dictatorships certainly did not invent this coupling of rationality and religiosity. All ideologically informed social movements of mass character involve some combining of these elements. But Hitler and Stalin were original in the sense of deliberately plotting the combination and then preserving it in a usable balance through the quest for power and its subsequent exercise in governance. Nor is it my contention that this combination, or the urge toward thought control implicit in it, suffices without a number of other instruments and mechanisms to bring a "totalitarian" movement to power; the point is rather the opposite, namely that this approach enables us to identify totalitarian tendencies in timely fashion instead of merely describing them as such after their realization has made resistance all but impossible. Also, I am using the term "religiosity" to designate an unleashed irrationalism that, however much it may reflect <u>some</u> system of religious belief, is not necessarily inclusive of or even compatible with institutionalized religious doctrine or observance. Finally, it would not do to leave uncorrected the possible conclusion that all attempts to inculcate belief systems--whether we call them education, indoctrination, propaganda, or ideology--are <u>ipso facto</u> to be branded as totalitarian. The refinement of this portion of the argument can best be done under the heading of human freedom, the third term of our title.

* * * * * * * *

To be warranted as a distinct concept, "totalitarianism," as I have so far argued, must at least capture what is exceptional about the two cases that awakened the need for a new concept. It ought also to have room in it for similar threats in different trappings, and should, if it is to be serviceable in a preventive sense, be applicable to movements and potential rulers before they actually secure power.

Conventional autocracies have commonly availed themselves of the other instruments (or, as in the case of advanced technology, of their historical cognates) of absolute power as these appear in enumerative definitions of totalitarianism. But they have not typically cared very much what their subjects thought so long as outward obedience was assured. The movements and regimes that we want to distinguish from ordinary autocracy by calling them totalitarian care a great deal about the thoughts and beliefs of their citizens. Ideologically freighted and gripped by a perverse notion of purpose and perfectibility, they are uneasy about anything that falls short of total commitment and loyalty. My argument has taken two routes to reach this position: the first, suggested indirectly by <u>Torstenson</u>, to the effect that totalitarianism unites a morally unconstrained rationality and irrational mass fervor, precisely the qualities that remain separate and mutually opposed in ordinary dictatorship; and the second that claims a singular or extraordinary status, at least as an identifying emblem of totalitarianism, for the impulse to control the content of people's minds. These two routes intersect,

as I have already hinted, because a movement
or regime that enlists mass participation and
seeks to keep popular fervor mobilized in
behalf of its program cannot leave to chance
the forces, the urges, or the objectives that
might galvanize contrary mass sentiment
within the subject population. And this
implies the need to control thought as well
as action, not just through suasion but by
utilizing, as need dictates, the whole armory
of coercion. The dictator (tyrant, despot)
is one who monopolizes the instruments of
coercion; the happy dictator (totalitarian
ruler or leader)is one who has reached, or
can reasonably hope to reach, the point of
not needing to use them.

We are brought now into direct
confrontation with the multifaceted problem
of religion and, at one further remove, the
problem of human freedom in relation to
totalitarianism. Religion and freedom were
plainly linked when the Barmen Synod rejected
the pretensions of Nazi doctrine, as they are
when the Lithuanian Catholics or the Russian
Baptists enter into resistance against
official Soviet ideology. Taken in their
widest meanings, however, religion and human

freedom are not automatically or
self-evidently conjoined, and the worthy
impulse to celebrate acts of resistance
rooted in religious conviction surely
requires that we distinguish resistance from
the other roles that religion can play in
confrontation with totalitarian claims.

Religion in its organized, institutional
forms offers two more or less equally
challenging postures in relation to the
pretensions of totalitarianism: it is at
once a belief system and a social
institution, both antedating and thus not
automatically beholden to a new regime.
Ultimately, the belief system has to count as
an affront to totalitarian claims; the church
as social institution may also, or it may
not, depending on its tractability. We are
dealing, of course, with a process, not a
static situation, and strategy may dictate
wide spectra of persecution or accommodation.

The particularities of our two cases may
help at this point. Neither regime exhibited
much tolerance for either aspect of religion
that stood in the way of consolidating power.
The Bolsheviks undertook much more overt

action against churches, observances, and
religious beliefs initially, in keeping with
the Leninist view (not to be confused with
Marx's own, by the way)[14] that religious
belief could and should be coerced out of
existence and also, of course, on the
plausible assumption that the church was part
of the class enemy. Hitler's early moves
were governed more by tactical considerations
and might best be characterized as a gradual
undermining of both the intellectual and
institutional foundations of organized
religion. Both Stalin and Hitler showed
themselves quite capable of strategic
accommodation--as when Stalin saw Orthodoxy,
rather fully domesticated by that time
anyway, as an instrument of popular
mobilization in the face of impending war.
Hitler rather consciously adopted a veneer of
religious observance and Stalin somewhat more
inadvertently imparted a religious flavor to
proceedings meant to be secular in nature.
In the final analysis, at any rate, both
aimed to substitute official party doctrine
for the teachings of the churches. In
effect, one might say, Hitler meant to found
a Nazi church infused with a doctrine
perfectly congruent with Nazi teachings;

Stalin meant to extirpate religion and ended up with party ceremonial that looked suspiciously liturgical. "In its own fashion," as Milosz says, "the Party too is a church."[15] Although the anti-religious stance of Bolshevism was always the more overt and insistent, the basic proposition holds that both regimes had to regard any vestige of authentic, preexistent religious conviction as hostile competition in the realm of belief.

Turning the coin over and viewing matters from the standpoint of the church or of the believer, there was no choice in the Bolshevik case but to be in opposition. Whether or not this resulted in acts of resistance, the victorious party had condemned both religious institutions and religious belief as counterrevolutionary forces. Later on, though perhaps only temporarily, Orthodoxy (but not Judaism or other Christian confessions) had the option of preserving itself through complicity. In Hitler's Germany, the Christian churches had the option of complicity all along (Judaism, of course, did not) and, like their Orthodox cousins, mostly took it. Ultimately it was

impossible under either regime for the
religiously convinced to suppose that their
posture would be tolerated in the long run.
All might choose between active and passive
resistance (and the latter should not be too
lightly discounted by those of us who have
not experienced totalitarianism directly),
but the deepest irony of all, perhaps, is that
the Jews of Germany and all of the faithful
under early Bolshevism were denied the choice
between complicity and resistance and hence
the privilege of joining the morally
non-complicit "saving remnant."

It should be clear by now that religious
institutions and their members could play
different roles in the two historical
episodes that we know as totalitarian. One
possibility, exemplified by Barmen, was to
resist. Another was to accommodate and
become, almost automatically, an instrument
of the regime's program--which was the course
taken by most who had that option. (Barmen
should not blind us to the prevailing
supineness of the German churches, nor should
it lead us to ignore socialists, trade
unionists, and others whose resistance to
Hitler was at least as steadfast and often

more energetic.)[16] A third possibility, arising sometimes out of persuasion and sometimes out of opportunism, was effective apostasy--transferring religious sentiment and energy (what I have meant by "religiosity") to the enemy and thus becoming an enthusiastic rather than a reluctant agent of the official cult.

If these were the possible religious stances vis-à-vis totalitarianism, we arrive at our concluding questions: what kind of freedom do we want to espouse and where does religion fit in the effort to realize it?

* * * * * *

It is doubtless possible to hold that the political differences among individuals who divide roughly into conservatives and progressives are rooted in temperamental differences: optimists tend to be more progressive in outlook, pessimists are likelier to be conservative in orientation. On the intellectual plane, where convictions are worked out in full seriousness and ideas are seen as guides to action, it is probably better to speak of beliefs about human nature. Those who hold a skeptical or pessimistic view of human nature tend, in approximate correspondence to the temperamental pessimists, to settle for modest social goals and a negative notion of human freedom. Those who are more sanguine about human nature, matching up to the optimists by temperament, are apt to favor ambitious social objectives and a positive approach to freedom. The negative view of freedom, defensive and individualistic, identifies an enemy, usually government, and seeks protection against encroachments on individual rights by the enemy. The positive approach to freedom, while in no way excluding such defenses against encroachment, regards authentic freedom as a social attainment wherein individuals realize their potentialities in human communities. Negative freedom is a defense of what we already possess; or, when losses occur, it is an attempt to recover what we once had. Positive freedom is the urge to go beyond anything yet realized, to fulfill human capacities that can only be glimpsed as potentialities.

The twentieth century has not been kind to the positive view. Resurgent xenophobia, barbarism in the heart of Christendom, recurrent genocide, and the ultimate form of domination, thought control (here proposed as the hallmark of totalitarianism) all combine to justify the pessimist as realistic and anathematize the optimist as utopian. What more proof do we need that human nature is at best divided and at worst depraved, that modest social goals are the only realistic ones, and that ambitious programs for the species are fated to turn sour? The modern world is one in which those inhabiting the daring social experiments look with envy upon their brothers and sisters who settled for less ambitious social goals and concentrated on the preservation of at least an approximation of individual liberty. Totalitarianism, one might say, has given ambition a bad name.

But do we then want to range all those who resist tyranny in its modern totalitarian form on the side of modest realism? Are the churchmen of the Barmen Synod, the anti-Hitler conspirators of 1944, Franz Jägerstätter, the socialists in exile,

Trotsky, the Baptists of Soviet Russia, authentic Marxist critics of Stalinism, and the assorted guerillas and ghetto-fighters caught between Hitler and Stalin all to be enlisted in support of a negative defense of human freedom? Some of the aforementioned were undoubtedly political conservatives (a perfectly good basis for resisting tyranny, of course), and some were certainly animated by personal moral commitments or by salvationist understandings that were largely irrelevant (or only symbolically relevant) socially. But it is by no means clear that all of the resistors would themselves have been comfortable as defenders of a merely negative view of human freedom, still less as defenders of any particular status quo. It is a tribute to none of them to rest a contemporary triumphalism of any sort on their examples. We would be according an ironic and totally undeserved victory to vanquished totalitarianisms, as well as defaming many of their victims, were we to permit the horrifying capabilities they disclosed to drive us into complacency about the liberties we do possess or pessimism about the quest for a larger vision of freedom and justice.

As totalitarianism is ambitious and ordinary autocracy modest, a negative version of freedom, being also modest, suggests a stronger safeguard against totalitarianism, whereas programs of social transformation (positive freedom), being ambitious, hint at an opening of the gates to totalitarian outcomes. Although it is undeniable that ambitious social movements have sometimes been bent to totalitarian objectives, it is also undeniable that the mass following available to totalitarian movements is generated by disenchantment with the modest approaches to freedom and social change that usually equate to some variety of class privilege. The allure of the cautious defense of the status quo is thus illusory: it reflects a deceptive analogy favorable to modesty and conceals the manner in which an unsatisfactory status quo feeds the very preconditions of totalitarianism. Without a mass following imbued with religious fervor and prepared to abdicate critical judgment in yielding to cultist, ideological direction, the threats to human freedom would look like Torstenson, not like Hitler or Stalin. Not a delightful prospect perhaps, it is certainly a more manageable one than the phenomena that occasioned this entire problematic in the first place.

Authentic religion, let us also remember, is invariably ambitious as well. Unlike civil religion, which is accommodationist and therefore conservative, genuine religious sentiment always embraces large imperatives as routes to salvation beyond history and quite often as prerequisites of an acceptable communitarian existence within history. This contrast between modest civil religion and ambitious religion of discipline and authenticity is one of the ways of characterizing the difference between the Barmen Synod and the overall record of the German churches under Hitler. And it would serve equally well to distinguish the resisting forms of religion in Eastern Europe--Christian, Judaic, Islamic, and even pagan--from the intrumentalized institutions that pacify their congregations as they apologize for the regime.[17]

Attempting now to draw the strands of my argument together, I must underscore the

multidimensionality of all three items of the
title. If there is a simple relationship to
be found anywhere in the complexity of their
interrelationships, it is the
straightforward opposition between
totalitarianism and human freedom.
Totalitarianism is characterized in its most
salient feature by the urge and need to
curtail freedom in an ultimate way, by
effectuating a prior and even cheerful
obedience in the realm of thought and belief;
totalitarian tendencies are at their most
discernible when they manifest a coercive
approach to thought and belief. The defense
of human freedom, or of whatever measure of
freedom may have been attained, and all
efforts aimed at widening the realization of
human potential for freedom, are to be found
standing squarely in the path of totalitarian
dispositions, and they continue to assert
themselves, however falteringly, against a
totalitarianism in power.

Religion, on the other hand, stands in
an ambiguous relationship to both
totalitarianism and human freedom. The
vaguer sense of religion that I have called
popular fervor or religiosity may resist to

the death or it may be available in all its
energy to the statist cult. Institutional
religion may oppose, impede, support, or
collapse into totalitarian movements or
systems of rule. Although churches may be
ultimately incompatible with any full-blown
totalitarianism, at least if they maintain
even a shred of doctrinal integrity and
internal discipline, they do not always or
necessarily recognize that fact and may,
especially at the intermediate stages of
totalitarian development, resort to
compromise and complicity for the sake of
preserving themselves institutionally.
Finally, we must consider the worst thinkable
scenario from the standpoint of human
freedom: that organized religion could
itself generate a totalitarianism. In common
with all doctrinally-informed movements with
ambitious goals for humankind and its
communities, churches are tempted to move
from suasion to coercion in matters of
belief.[18] They have in their extreme
theocratic moments embodied conspicuous
totalitarian tendencies and might conceivably
pose a genuine totalitarian threat, not least
because they would, predictably, wear

trappings quite different from those that we have so far learned to fear.

When a Barmen Synod placed itself squarely athwart the totalitarian pretensions of its government, the situation was almost (but not quite) the obverse of a religious threat to freedom. Whether that oppositional stand was taken in defense of the church or in defense of human freedom, the effect was the same and it behooved nonbelievers to welcome it as an ally. It never becomes entirely irrelevant which purpose the resistance serves, and a clue is sometimes given, especially after the fact, when an oppositional exclusivity is asserted, denying, for example, the equal heroism and timeliness of resistance by socialists and communists (who may, of course, exhibit the very same tendency in evaluating the role of church resistance). The Soviet case is the same in that some forms of dissent originate with people who would, given the opportunity, in turn suppress freedom for others. Hence the need for constant concern and watchfulness as regards ultimate purposes. But at the crucial junctures, the neuralgic points in a struggle against totalitarianism, it is enough that resistance be manifested, for at that moment human freedom and the integrity of the religious institution are, as at Barmen, congruent if not identical objectives.

Absent an immediate totalitarian threat, the relation of religion, more specifically of religious liberty, to human freedom is if anything more problematical. Defenders of religious liberty sometimes claim, usually on the strength of either a natural rights or social contract conception of social order, that religion is prior and therefore in principle impervious to political arrangements that surround religious institutions. Constitutions and bills of rights that guarantee the freedom of religious belief and observance are thus seen as acknowledging prior rights, not creating them. On such a view, we get an absolutized principle of religious liberty, one that is immune to political or social intervention, not because a constitution interposes certain constraints, but because a constitution recognizes a prior and higher claim.

Now the nonbeliever who is not wedded to natural rights or social contract doctrine, but who is yet a steadfast devotee of human freedom, may well decide that guarantees of religious liberty are valuable--both because they fend off secular tendencies toward the coercion of belief and because the integrity of religious institutions affords important social supports in moments of crisis. That is a prudential defense of religious liberty but one that also withholds assent from an absolutized form of the principle. The point of the reservation is not, of course, that religious citizens are entitled to less than a fair share of civic protection, but that they have only the same entitlements as other citizens. The other side of the coin is that religious institutions are potentially just as dangerous to a postulated healthy, democratic polity, must be watched just as closely, and may have to be judged as severely as any other ambitious doctrinal program. I have already suggested that the experience of totalitarianism ought not to frighten us into such a cautious posture, defending negative freedom, and therewith the status quo, while ambitious, positive visions of human potentiality are exiled from the

marketplace.   But the religious varieties of
those ambitious programs are not entitled,
either on the historical record or in the
logic of a modern political community, to a
privileged status.   In this perspective, the
Barmen Synod earns even higher marks than it
could as an exercise of prior privilege, for
it exemplifies, as few other events have done,
the possible congruence of religious
obligation and civic responsibility.

Footnotes

1. Frankfurt am Main, 1972; Meisel's epilogue, dated 1971, is entitled "After 45 Years," pp. 301-2.

2. Habermas's works are widely available in English; the most pertinent one here is probably <u>Theory and Practice</u> (Boston: Beacon Press, 1974), chapter 7.

3. See Hans Gerth and C. Wright Mills (eds.): <u>From Max Weber: Essays in Sociology</u> (New York: Oxford, 1946), chapter 8.

4. Bureaucracy has become such a convenient whipping boy--for its alleged parasitism when right-wing critics are speaking, for conservatism and unresponsiveness when left-wing critics have the floor--that it is necessary to remind both of the historic role of bureaucracy in substituting regularity and predictability for the arbitrariness of personal rule.

5. This is admittedly not a very precise concept but can be examined in its medieval and early modern manifestations in Europe in Norman Cohn: <u>The Pursuit of the Millennium</u> (New York: Harper, 1961); it is seldom if ever possible to disentangle religious motivations and

social discontent in peasant uprisings and rebellions of the sort that Meisel depicts.

6. The excessive use of anticommunist ideology in ostensible justification of U.S. foreign policy and defense budgets has allowed us to forget what a palpable threat Stalinism was in the postwar years, though even then our anticommunist zealots worried more about supposed internal perils than about the real hardships that were being visited upon Soviet citizens and neighboring peoples. The great irony of ideological anticommunism is that it supports Stalin's own claim, vigorously disputed by most Marxists, socialists, and serious revolutionaries, that he was entitled to speak authoritatively for those viewpoints.

7. One of the more satisfactory treatments is Hans Buchheim: Totalitarian Rule; Its Nature and Characteristics (Middle-town, Conn.: Wesleyan University Press, 1968), especially helpful on the matter of terminological antecedents. He does not mention the extent to which "Totalitarismus" was used, for example by members of the Institute for Social Research (Frankfurt School), in describing Nazism. But it remains true that the postwar American meaning prevailed when the term reappeared in postwar Germany.

8. See note #6, above; also, Czeslaw Milosz: The Captive Mind (New York: Vintage, 1981).

9. Hannah Arendt's book, <u>The Origins of Totalitarianism</u> (New York: Harcourt Brace, 2nd enl. ed., 1958), first appeared in 1951 but seems to have remained outside the mainstream of the academic discussion that followed. Her historical approach, though not highly esteemed by academic historians, seems to me in no way inferior to the predominant political science approach, less precise perhaps but possibly more illuminating. Friedrich may have had most to do with setting the tone of the scholarly discussion; see note 7, above, and note 10, below.

10. Carl J. Friedrich and Zbigniew K. Brzezinski: <u>Totalitarian Dictatorship and Autocracy</u> (Cambridge: Harvard University Press, 1956), p. 9: "The basic features or traits which we suggest as generally recognized to be common to totalitarian dictatorships are six in number. The 'syndrome,' or pattern of interrelated traits, of the totalitarian dictatorship consists of an ideology, a single party typically led by one man, a terroristic police, and communications monopoly, a weapons monopoly, and a centrally directed economy." It is admitted that the last two are common in non-totalitarian systems; also (p. 10) that the enumeration "is not meant to suggest that there might not be others, now insufficiently recognized..."

11. I do not mean to detract in any way from the heroism of, say, a Franz Jägerstätter, who refused out of religious conviction to serve Hitler's

regime. The symbolic importance of his refusal was great, but it was not a fundamental blow to the regime any more than regicide is a fundamental blow to monarchy. See Gordon C. Zahn: <u>In Solitary Witness: the Life and Death of Franz Jägerstätter</u> (New York: Holt, Rinehart and Winston, 1964).

12. See note 10, above.

13. For critical perspectives on the treatment of mental illness, see the works of R.D. Laing and Thomas Szasz. My use of the model in this way is not to be confused with a deliberate, malevolent misuse of mental institutions as auxiliaries of the Soviet penal system. See Sidney Bloch and Peter Reddaway: <u>Psychiatric Terror</u> (New York: Basic Books, 1977). yet the two phenomena are related in the sense that mastery of arcane knowledge confers a decisive edge to the professional over against the patient, not only in the person-to-person dimension but also in the way the external world tends to weigh testimony when views conflict. This is what makes psychiatry so convenient as a tool of Soviet proceedings against dissidents.

14. Marx never recommended coercive measures against religious belief, only against churches or any other social institutions that might count as forces of counterrevolution. Lenin apparently believed, on the other hand, that coercive acts against religious belief itself were in order. The whole problematic is developed more fully in

my "Marx, Marxism, and Religion,"
Forschungen zur osteuropäischen
Geschichte, 20, Berlin, 1973, pp.
35-55.

15. The Captive Mind, p. 207. This book
     appeared in 1953 to mark Milosz's break
     with the Polish government and party; it
     was reissued after Milosz was awarded
     the Nobel Prize for literature. It is
     still unsurpassed in its portrayal of
     Soviet actions in the early postwar
     period and also noteworthy for its
     refusal, uncommon in the literature of
     this field, to conflate Marxism and
     official communist doctrine. The quoted
     line appears near the beginning of the
     best account I know of the relation
     between Stalinist ideology and religion,
     art, and intellectual life in general,
     pp. 205 ff.

16. A standard work on the whole of the
     German resistance, Peter Hoffmann: The
     History of the German Resistance,
     1933-1945, (Cambridge: MIT Press,
     1977), is a chastening reminder, by its
     allocation of coverage, that the
     churches occupied a fairly modest place
     in the resistance. For a devastating
     critique of the German Church in
     relation to the Holocaust, see Franklin
     H. Littell: The Crucifixion of the
     Jews, (New York: Harper and Row,
     1974).

17. To this must be added that in Eastern
     Europe and many parts of the Soviet
     Union itself religion and nationality
     are so inextricably bound up with each
     other that it would be misleading to

suppose that religious dissent is the exclusive product of piety, devoutness, or church discipline. The current role of the Polish church is a particularly good illustration.

18. Here I refer to the theocratic tendency that intends to embrace all of society, not to an internal ethic that binds members to institutional discipline so long as they elect to retain membership.

CONTRIBUTORS

JOSEPH D. BETTIS is Professor at Western Washington University where he teaches religion and philosophy. A native of Texas, he received his Ph.D. from Princeton University and has taught at the University of Alabama and the University of Nebraska at Omaha. Author of several major essays on Karl Barth, he is editor of the widely popular college text, The Phenomenology of Religion.

JOHN S. CONWAY is Professor of History at the University of British Columbia. A native of England and educated at Cambridge where he received his Ph.D., Professor Conway has taught at the University of Manchester and St. John's College, is author of historical essays in Yad Vashem Studies, the Canadian Journal of History, Reconciliation Quarterly and the definitive study of the German Church Struggle in English, The Nazi Persecution of the Churches, 1933-45 (Basic Books, 1968).

ROBERT P. ERICKSEN teaches history at Olympia College in Bremerton, Washington and holds his Ph.D. from the London School of Economics and Political Science. Author of numerous papers and articles on Protestant theology during the Nazi era, his book Theologians Under Hitler is scheduled to be published by Yale University Press in 1984.

LYMAN H. LEGTERS is Professor of Russian and East European History at the University of Washington and a Senior Fellow of the William O. Douglas Institute. He received his Ph.D. from the Free University of Berlin and is editor of The German Democratic Republic, Marxism and the Good Society, and Western Society After the Holocaust.

HUBERT G. LOCKE is Professor and Dean, Graduate School of Public Affairs, University of Washington and Director of the William O. Douglas Institute. He is co-editor (with F. H. Littell) of The German Church Struggle and the Holocaust and coordinator for the International Symposium of Scholars and Church Leaders on "A Half-Century After Barmen."

TORONTO STUDIES IN THEOLOGY